Rethinking Faith

A Constructive Practical Theology

James Newton Poling

FORTRESS PRESS
Minneapolis

*Dedicated to my teacher, Allen Moore, who introduced me
to practical theology and supported me throughout my
development as a practical theologian*

RETHINKING FAITH
A Constructive Practical Theology

Unless otherwise noted, scripture quotations are the author's own translation or from the New
Revised Standard Version Bible, copyright © 1989 by the Division of Christian Education of
the National Council of Churches of Christ in the USA, and are used with permission.

"Good News for Modern Man, Bad News for Modern Women," by Larraine Frampton, pp. 48–49,
is used by permission of the author.

Cover image and design: Joe Vaughan
Book design: Timothy W. Larson, Minneapolis, MN

Library of Congress Cataloging-in-Publication Data

Poling, James N. (James Newton), 1942–
  Rethinking faith : a constructive practical theology / James Newton Poling.
     p. cm.
  Includes bibliographical references and (p.   ) index.
  ISBN 978–0–8006–9754–9 (alk. paper)
1. Theology, Doctrinal. 2. Practical theology. I. Title.
  BT78.P653 2011
  230—dc22   2011015060

The paper used in this publication meets the minimum requirements of Amercan National
Standard for Information Sciences—Permanence of Paper for Printed Library Materials, ANSI
Z329.48-1984.

Manufactured in the U.S.A.
15   14   13   12   11   1   2   3   4   5   6   7   8   9   10

Contents

Acknowledgments

How can I give credit to the people who have influenced me over forty years of ministry? I must begin with my parents, Newton and Virginia Poling, my wife, Nancy Werking Poling, and my children, Christie and Nathan, my in-laws, and my six grandchildren from whom I have learned a lot about life. Nancy, especially, has been my best critic, my editor, and my partner in many projects. Many congregations, denominations, and theological schools have influenced me. I especially thank Garrett-Evangelical Theological Seminary for their generosity for the last fifteen years as they supported my teaching and research. I have had many valuable colleagues. I taught the seminar in practical theology with Jeffery Tribble and Jack Seymour, and learned much from my faculty friends in pastoral theology, Lallene Rector, David Hogue, and Pamela Holliman. Jack Seymour, Larry Graham, and Christie Neuger read portions of this manuscript and gave me important feedback. I thank students for the privilege of teaching and learning together. I especially thank Linda Crockett and Philip who represent the many survivors of violence I have journeyed with. Brenda Ruiz, my colleague in Managua, Nicaragua, has accompanied me as I struggled to understand the world outside the United States. Faculty and students at Yonsei University School of Theology have introduced me to Korean and Asian ways of thinking and living the Christian faith. I thank my colleagues of the Society for Pastoral Theology, the American Association of Practical Theology, and the International Academy of Practical Theology, who have all encouraged and challenged my research. God has sent me many teachers and co-pilgrims, and I am thankful for them all. To God be honor and praise.

Introduction

What is the nature of God as revealed in the communities that follow Jesus Christ and what practices best express faith in God? This is a
question of practical theology. In this book, I respond to this question
on three levels: first, as a practical
theologian; second, as a baptized
member of the Christian church;
and, third, as a follower of Jesus
Christ in solidarity with those who
have suffered violence in their lives.
In the following section, I address
these three levels of theological
reflection about the nature of God:
(1) Practical theology and the nature of God; (2) Christian life and the
nature of God; and (3) Surviving violence and the nature of God.

> What is the nature of God as
> revealed in the communities
> that follow Jesus Christ and
> what practices best express
> faith in God?

THREE LEVELS OF THEOLOGICAL REFLECTION

*1. What does practical theology contribute to the theological disciplines and
the church about the nature of God in Jesus Christ?*
    Practical theology is a discipline of theological reflection that gives
sustained attention to the movement of God's Spirit in the everyday
lives of contemporary Christian communities for the sake of more

faithful practices. In dialogue with biblical, historical, and systematic theological reflection, practical theologians ask questions about God's ongoing self-revelation through the witness of faithful believers. Out of this reflection comes wisdom and programs that inform the church and the theological conversations among scholars and church leaders.[1]

In recent decades, practical theologians have written many essays about the methods by which we understand religious experience and God's actions in human lives.[2] As a result, practical theology has gained recognition as a branch of theology alongside biblical, historical, and systematic branches. However, establishing practical theology as a method of theology appropriate for academic research does not answer some important questions: What do practical theologians have to say about God in Jesus Christ? If God speaks through the practices of communities of faith, what do practical theologians have to contribute to the doctrinal content of the theologies of the churches?

As a practical theologian, I believe that everyday practices of following Jesus Christ lead to revelation about the nature of God. That is, persons and communities who believe in Jesus Christ and dedicate themselves to following "the Jesus way" in their lives will be touched by God's love and power so that new witness emerges. This new witness will have continuity with the long history of God's self-revelation through Scripture, history, and theology. But it will contribute new ideas and new practices as part of the ongoing conversation about God and God's will for humankind in the present and future. I believe that while God's character is consistent with past self-revelations, God's interaction with the world continues today and tomorrow. Given the limits of human faith and understanding, the scope of God's revelation is far beyond what we know, and novel forms of revelation are always happening if we pay attention.

> What do practical theologians have to say about God in Jesus Christ?

The idea that God's revelation is ongoing and not completed in Scripture is a contested idea among believers and theologians.[3] As a believer in the Reformed Protestant tradition, I believe that the Scriptures are the necessary revelation of God in Christ, and that the history of reflections of Christian communities in creeds and doctrines are authoritative for Christian life. I also believe that the reformation of the church continues because God has more to say about the nature of love and power as humans are ready to hear it. *Ecclesia reformata, semper reformanda*—that is, "The church reformed, always reforming."[4] Every day is a new challenge for believers to understand God, and God is actively trying to reach us with new understandings that fit our changed situations.

Within this project, my dialogue partners outside of practical theology will be in biblical and systematic theology. I focus especially on narratives of the Hebrew Bible and the Gospels as informed by feminist and liberation theology. Within systematic theology, my home is in process theology, an American theology that has grown in conversation with the philosophical perspectives of Alfred North Whitehead and other process philosophers. The reader will find frequent references to writers and ideas from these perspectives in my witness.[5]

2. What is the nature of the trinitarian God and the ecclesial witness to Jesus Christ in the world?

According to the long witness of Hebrew and Christian communities, God is faithful in the midst of the creative adventure of human life on planet earth. Scripture is a narrative of human surprise and shock at God's word in particular situations. Human self-deception distorts efforts to comprehend God's character and God's will as it unfolds within history. Theology throughout history has too often become a form of distorted human self-understanding that hides rather than reveals the mission of God in history. One of my assumptions is that normative claims of theology must always be tested within the crucible of everyday human life and faith. For Christians, human life depends on the constant presence of God's love and power. Discerning the nature of God's presence and will is critical to human survival and flourishing. In this sense theology is not primarily an academic discipline, but the struggle of believers and believing communities to understand and conform to God's presence in their everyday lives.

> What is the witness of believers and believing communities about God's presence in their everyday lives?

In order to explore the constructive contributions of practical theology to Christian doctrines, I have organized this book into several

traditional categories of systematic theology—God, sin and evil, Christology, Holy Spirit and church, eschatology, and practices of faith. In
each of these sections I share my witness to God in Jesus Christ based
on my study of the Scriptures, and the tradition, as well as my study
of practices of faithfulness within communities of faith. As a believer
and a scholar, I confess my personal faith and also engage in conversation with other believers and scholars. The result is a beginning of a
personal, constructive, systematic practical theology about the nature
of God in Christ that is meant for believers and practicing Christians as
well as scholars and theologians of the church. Those who are skeptical
of the Christian faith may find my theological reformulation interesting because the ideas may take a different perspective from traditional
Christians on the nature of human religious life.

*3. What can the church learn about the love and power of God in Jesus
Christ from the community of survivors of violence?*
     All theology is shaped by particular life situations. Theologians
must be confessional about the particular communities that create the
reference point for their reflections. My faith is particularly shaped by
those who have been victims and abusers of domestic violence and other
forms of violence such as racism, genocide, and colonial oppression.
Some Christian survivors of violence describe experiences of descending
into hell and meeting Jesus Christ who empowered them to survive,
heal, and thrive. Out of their faith these witnesses have proclaimed religious insights for modern times. As I have journeyed with survivors of
violence, I have come to the conviction that through these survivors
God is revealing important truth in our time about the nature of human
violence and the resilient love of God that empowers the church to be
faithful.
     My faith is also shaped by persons who have sexually abused others
and sought healing and accountability for their sin. Sexual offenses are
highly stigmatized in the United States; therefore, understanding the
interior spirituality of persons who have abused others is an urgent and
difficult task. I believe that the resilient spirit of some abusers reveals the
resilient love and power of God.[6]
     Victims of violence and those who use violence against others have
existed throughout Christian history, but only recently have their voices
been heard as a public witness to God's love and power. This is not the

first time that such a new religious witness has arisen in the history of the church. Believers who met Jesus on earth believed that they participated in a new revelation about the nature of God's love and power. Their New Testament witness to God in Jesus Christ has inspired many believers through history. Likewise, in many previous eras believers claimed that their lives were transformed through personal encounters with Jesus through faith.[7] In this book I am asking a practical theological question: What is the witness of Christian survivors of violence to the trinitarian God, and how do we understand their ecclesial witness to Jesus Christ in the world?

> What is the witness of Christian survivors of violence to God and to Jesus Christ in the world?

PERSONAL DISCLOSURE

I grew up in the liberal wing of the Reformed tradition as interpreted by the Anabaptist and Pietist communities.[8] My father was a pastor in the Church of the Brethren in Virginia and Maryland during my formative years, and I learned orthodox Reformed trinitarian doctrine with a special emphasis on community service, pacifism, and social justice. My mother was the daughter of a pastor. She worked for several years for the progressive national office of the Church of the Brethren during the time when they organized relief efforts in Spain during its civil war and lobbied with the government for conscientious-objector status for members of our denomination in anticipation of World War II. As a young adult, my theology of nonviolence and social concern was re-formed in the U.S. civil rights and peace movements of the 1960s. After almost a decade of pastoral ministry, I moved into graduate theological education and became an advocate of process theology. In graduate school, I was strongly influenced by feminist, liberation, and gay theologies. I have studied practical and pastoral theology and counseling in the United States, Europe, Central America, and Asia, and I have written about intercultural understandings of the gospel. I am currently a retired minister of Word and Sacrament in the Presbyterian Church (U.S.A.). All of these various religious influences have brought me back home to my childhood faith: How can I understand the trinitarian God of love and power who teaches community service, justice, and nonviolence in a complex world of beauty and terror?

I have personal reasons for my concern with human violence. I was born in the United States during World War II, raised in a pacifist tradition, nurtured in the nonviolent resistance of the civil rights movement, and shaped by my work as a pastoral counselor in the prevention of domestic violence movement. The contradiction between the love and power of God on the one hand and the consequences of human violence on the other hand troubles me greatly. I have spent much of my ministry working with abusers and survivors of violence. Through the resilient love of survivors and the courageous spiritual quest of some abusers, I have come to believe that salvation and healing from the effects of violence is possible through the grace of God. Two persons have become especially important influences, and they will be present in many of the chapters that follow. Linda Crockett survived child abuse by her mother and became a significant community leader in the prevention of domestic violence movement; Linda and I have journeyed together for fifteen years. Philip (a pseudonym) has suffered a life-long depression based on deprivations of his childhood and social oppression. As an adult, he abused his power by sexually molesting two adolescent boys. We have journeyed together for twenty-five years through many challenges of his life.

During some periods, the churches have courageously stood with survivors of violence and made a strong witness against the abuses of the powerful. At other periods, the church has compromised its witness to Jesus Christ by choosing abusive power over love and healing. In a post–9/11 world, the churches have an opportunity to be witnesses to the nonviolent love of Christ and the resilient hope that comes from faith in God.

This book is a summary of my own witness after more than sixty years of discipleship to Jesus Christ. My personal creed, provided below, contains a summary of my beliefs from my personal life and professional ministry. Every candidate for ministry in the Presbyterian Church (U.S.A.) is required to write and defend a brief statement of faith. Several times I have been questioned by groups of representative Presbyterian believers in order to be approved for ordained ministry. My statement of faith is in my denominational tradition. The chapters following the statement of faith further articulate my theology. I hope to give a convincing presentation of what I believe is most true about God in Jesus Christ as a contribution to the larger conversation about the nature of God within the Christian churches.

TO THE READERS

The blend of faith practices and scholarship in this book could be helpful for any thoughtful Christian as he or she develops a theology that is both personal and conversant with other voices. Indeed, I encourage leaders of faithful communities everywhere to engage in the discipline of uncovering the implicit theologies at work in your communities and articulating them for a wider public conversation. In this way, we give voice to the hidden things that God consistently communicates to humans but are often blocked by finitude and sin.

I invite the reader to join me on this journey. Our lives and faith are embedded in long histories and complex social situations. It is not simple to state our faith—God is complex and multifaceted; the world is complicated and confusing; we ourselves are inevitably ambiguous and contradictory. To find our way as human beings, we need ways of thinking and practices of faith that can help us keep our balance in the mist of uncertainty and violence.

Resilience and ambiguity have become important to me in my faith journey. Resilience refers to the indomitable will of human beings to find creative solutions in the midst of the deep contradictions of life. Ambiguity refers to the contradictions that confront human beings every day of our lives. I believe that resilience and ambiguity are built into creation and can be understood as part of God's character. These ideas give me hope that we

What is your witness to God in Christ and what evidence do you find in the practices of Christian communities?

humans can find our way in this world with God's help. This book is an attempt to summarize the way I have found so far. I hope my work will also empower you to summarize the way you have found.

A Personal Creed

I believe in God. I believe that the love and power of God, as revealed by Scripture, tradition, and religious experience, are best described as relational, ambiguous, and resilient. God is radically relational with the world. I understand relationality between God and the world as a process of interaction characterized by asymmetrical mutuality. God and the world are bound together in a web of mutuality that gives identity to each. God, the first person of the Trinity, constantly forms the world in its struggle for existence, meaning, and power. The world, in its responses to God, creates value that both enhances and diminishes the love and power of God. While this interchange is not symmetrical—that is, God's power and love is the foundation for the love and power of the world—God and humans depend on one another for responses that create identity and value.

Human beings are made in the image of God as loving and powerful. God calls humanity to exercise power in loving ways to advance the creative purposes of God. However, the history of human life shows that humans distort the image of God in their hearts and create institutions and ideologies that promote destruction of bodies, persons, and the ecology of the earth. Human sin becomes systemic evil that leads to abuse of power, violence, and the destruction of war and environmental catastrophe. Systemic evil promotes individual sin through apathy, sloth, greed, and other deadly sins. The problem of evil leads to the question of salvation: What cooperative work of God and humans will rescue the world from self-destruction and the loss of meaning, value, and beauty?

I believe in Jesus Christ, a divine and human being, who fully embodies the reality of God and humanity and discloses for humans both the character of God and the character of human life in the world. In the Scriptures, we see Jesus as a human being with extraordinary love and sensitivity for the full web of human and natural life. Because his attachment to life was shown in his actions of healing, teaching, and challenges to evil, Jesus was beloved by the people. Because of his truth telling and nonviolent symbolic confrontations of those with dominating power, he was crucified. Because of the resilient love and power of God, Jesus was resurrected and lives today to lure the faithful into communion with God and to reveal the stature of human life that is possible through communion with God. "Christ has died; Christ has risen; Christ will come again"—these liturgical words call us to embrace the historical reality and the real presence of Jesus Christ, the second member of the Trinity. Through Christ, humanity is healed from the ravages of evil and transformed for ministries with others. Jesus Christ revealed that God and humans are relational, ambiguous, and resilient in the midst of evil.

I believe in the Holy Spirit, the third person of the Trinity, who provides everyday empowerment for the world. The Spirit strengthens the resilience of human beings in the midst of the complex relationships and the moral ambiguity of daily life. The Holy Spirit redeems human and natural life. I believe the church is called to be the body of Christ, a community of bodies and spirits, of humans and nature, in communion with the Holy Spirit, with the following marks: (1) inclusive love, (2) empowering justice, (3) nonviolent resistance to evil, (4) multiplicity and unity, (5) ambiguity and goodness. Through worship, the sacraments of baptism and communion, and programs of care and prophetic witness, the true church creates a resilient witness of hope for a suffering world.

I believe in the eschaton, the telos of God's love and power, as an image of a harmonious community of peace and prosperity for all human and nonhuman beings, including the material world. The ritual saying, "Christ will come again," means that all creation groans for the beloved community that God intends. Jesus comes through the Spirit in every moment that the love and power of God are fully disclosed in reality. The hope for Jesus' coming in the future is a lure toward the harmony and beauty given by God for all creation.

ONE
The Forming God

*I believe in God. I believe that the love and power of God, as revealed
by Scripture, tradition, and religious experience, are best described as
relational, ambiguous, and resilient. God is radically relational with
the world. I understand relationality between God and the world
as a process of interaction characterized by asymmetrical mutuality.
God and the world are bound together in a web of mutuality that
gives identity to each. God, the first person of the Trinity, constantly
forms the world in its struggle for existence, meaning, and power. The
world, in its responses to God, creates value that both enhances and
diminishes the love and power of God. While this interchange is not
symmetrical—that is, God's power and love are the foundation for
the love and power of the world—God and humans depend on one
another for responses that create identity and value.*

Who is God and what are God's
intentions for the world? This is
the question of the first person of
the Trinity. If we understand God
as responsible for the direction of
the empirical reality of everyday life in partnership with God's creatures
who are free, what can we say about the character of God based on
Scripture, theology, and contemporary religious experience?

> Who is God and what are
> God's intentions for the
> world?

SCRIPTURE

Within Scripture, God is sometimes called Father,[1] by which the texts
often mean Creator, the one who made the world. In both creation
stories that appear in Genesis, God created the world into water, land,

plants, animals, persons, and social systems, and God said that it was good.[2] As an ancient text, the creation story of Genesis 1 is more compatible with modern scientific explanations because it suggests an evolutionary and progressive creation of structures from the simple to the more complex. Light and darkness are followed by water, then seas, rocks, simple living organisms, plants, fish, animals, and finally humans. In Genesis 1, God is like an engineer who organizes the world according to principles of science. Genesis 2 offers a more relational and poetic account of creation. God shapes human beings from clay, breathes life into them, and then creates animals and other persons as companions. In this story, God is like a midwife or artist who lovingly creates a world based on interpersonal relationships. In both stories, there is an asymmetrical mutuality between God and the world—God creates a world that operates by certain principles as an expression of God's basic identity; God is a God who creates; the world is the world because of its covenant with God. Divine and human destinies are tied together. God is angry and disappointed when the world does not fulfill its purpose; human beings are angry and disappointed when God is absent and withholds the love and power necessary for humans to thrive.

The book of Psalms can be read as a record of conversations between God and humans about their relationship. They are filled with love, admiration, praise, gratefulness, affection, and honor as well as hurt, guilt, shame, rage, and destructive thoughts—the full range of human thoughts and emotions. The psalms are often organized into categories such as praise, lament, and petition, although all three functions can be found in many psalms. For example, Psalm 100 is often taught to children because it contains strong praise images without any negative human feelings: "Enter his gates with thanksgiving, . . . for the Lord is good; his steadfast love endures forever, and his faithfulness to all generations." Walter Brueggemann calls these "psalms of orientation"[3] —praise for the goodness of God during times when particular human communities are stable and secure. Many Christian parents want their children to love God unreservedly and give God praise for the goodness of our lives together. It is a premise of Christian education that the church should establish a positive image of God early in life so that children and new Christians have a foundation to return to when they face challenges in life.

Psalms of lament express the pain of the human community in times of tragedy and oppression. Sometimes lament takes the form of rage at enemies and calls for God's revenge on them. One of the harshest is Psalm 137:8: "Doomed Babylon, be cursed! Good for those who deal you evil for evil! Good for those who destroy you, who smash your children at the walls."[4] At other times the lament takes the form of individual depression and a feeling that God is absent, such as Psalm 39:4-13: "LORD, let me know my end, . . . let me know how fleeting my life is. . . . Surely everyone goes about like a shadow. Surely for nothing they are in turmoil; . . . Turn your gaze away from me, that I may smile again, before I depart and am no more." In some laments, hope seems to be absent for the believer, except that lament is directed to God and therefore is a part of an ongoing conversation with God. But other laments have powerful images of hope in the midst of human suffering; for example, Psalm 30:11-12: "You have turned my mourning into dancing; you have taken off my sackcloth and clothed me with joy, so that my soul may praise you and not be silent. O LORD my God, I will give thanks to you forever." Lament psalms are resources that can provide comfort during times of loss and oppression because they give theological language to human feelings that need to be expressed. Implicitly, these psalms say that humans can bring everything to God in prayer without worry that we will be punished and rejected. Even the worst evil in human life is not outside the human relationship with God.

In the psalms of new orientation, there is an implied or explicit faith that God has saved us from suffering and oppression and restored the good life. Consider Psalm 66:16: "Come and hear, all you who fear God, and I will tell what he has done for me. I cried aloud to him, and he was extolled with my tongue. . . . But truly God has listened; he has given heed to the words of my prayer." The witness about "what God has done for me" has had powerful impact on the contemporary churches that practice testimonials. In many communities of faith, the people celebrate the God who has remained faithful in the "valley of the shadow of death" (Psalm 23). Praise of God that comes after tragedy and loss is often the most powerful expression of hope. Though I was lost, now I am found. The psalms are conversations with God that assume a real relationship, a partnership in which each has responsibilities and humans can call on God for redemption and rescue in the midst of oppression and affliction.

The narrative of the Scriptures is commentary on the asymmetrical relationship between God and humans. Immediately after the creation, the first humans engaged in deception and conspiracy against God to violate the limits of the created order. In a sense it doesn't matter what the limits were; what matters is that humans succumbed to the temptation to exceed them. Both animals and humans have power that can bring life and death, and humans have freedom to choose life or death. The biblical narrative describes the human struggle to choose life rather than death. The story points to life on the razor's edge between life and death, between beauty and boredom, between love and destructiveness. King David was chosen by God and the people because of his virtue and courage in the face of great danger, yet he chose evil when he took Bathsheba and killed Uriah and initiated generations of violence in his own family.[5] In the encounter with the evil he had done, David was repentant and redeemed although his repentance did not avoid the consequences of his sin for his family and his subjects. His recovery from sin and evil endeared him to the community that later gave him credit for authoring the psalms, the community's greatest prayerbook.

> What do the prayers called the psalms tell us about the character of God?

The story of the rise, fall, and redemption of David is a statement of a core theme of the Scriptures. The same formula is repeated in the story of the birth of Israel, its fall into disobedience, its corruption and injustice to the poor, its punishment in exile, and its restoration as a faithful nation. In this story, God and particular human communities live in mutual covenant with one another; their destinies are tied together. God and the human community are not affected in exactly the same way; for example, there is no indication that God will die, while humans are constantly faced with death. But there is a way that the quality of the divine-human relationship is significant for God as well as humans. God hopes that the human community will enrich the beauty of the world and is disappointed and experiences pain when humans decide to destroy beauty rather than sustain and create it. We cannot know how much any particular project like the history of the Jewish people means in the total life of God because we don't have access to the full reality of the transcendent God. But the Scriptures witness that God invests significant energy and concern in the stories of the Jewish people.

The Bible is the formative book for Christian faith and action. Many Christians believe the New Testament has a special authority and are not reticent to believe that its theology has universal significance. Most Christians believe that Jesus was more than just another prophet of the Word of God, that Jesus is the second person of the Trinity, and that Jesus' life is the decisive revelation of God to humans. Some theo-

> The sequence of "creation, fall, and redemption" is one way to understand the narrative of the Scriptures. How does this apply to your life?

ries of Christian evangelization of the world are based on the confidence that Christians have the final truth that is necessary for the salvation of the world. This can make interreligious dialogue highly problematic. Other Christians believe that while the gospel of Jesus Christ and the Scriptures are authoritative for Christian identity, the authority of revelation for Christians does not limit God to only one religion. Rather, they believe that God is an active force in all religions, revealing God's nature in multiple ways. Therefore, interreligious dialogue is crucial for a fuller understanding of the nature of God. Being christocentric can be exclusive (there are no other revelations outside of Christ) or inclusive (Christ has shaped our identity, and we are enriched by conversations with other religions).

According to most biblical interpretations, Jesus did not go through the formulaic developmental stages as originally virtuous, then fallen, then redeemed. A rough parallel is Jesus' election at his baptism, his crucifixion and descent into hell, and his resurrection on the third day. In these events, Jesus goes through the stages of human spiritual life, but without sin and without the full impact that such an experience would have for humans. There is little inclination within popular Christian thought for believers to see Jesus as fully human in spite of the ancient creeds.[6] Yet, seeing Jesus as fully human and fully divine is a central doctrine of all contemporary Christian churches.

PROCESS THEOLOGY

Within process theology, God is relational because of God's ontological function within the world. According to process thinker Alfred North

Whitehead, one of the basic principles of reality is Creativity, which is his name for the process by which experiences (actual entities, in technical language) come into momentary existence through syntheses of past relationships and pass their influence and values on to the future. This process of coming into existence and passing on is the most elemental reality of the world, according to Whitehead. A rough parallel is the fact that all humans are born, live, and die; Whitehead, however, suggests that this process of birth, life, and death occurs in each moment of our experience. Therefore, human beings are always in process, always changing. We are born, live, and die in a continuous series of moments that constitute identity and conservation of values.

One of Whitehead's central questions was, What is the principle that determines whether creativity results in increased value or continuous chaos? His answer: God is the being who influences the creation toward greater value. God is the one who sustains the values of goodness through the process that is always changing. Through an initial aim, God initiates each moment of experience and presents the graded possibilities that are available for synthesis in that moment. In this way, God helps to preserve the possibility of greater value (goodness) and to resist evil. Whether the maximum creation of value will occur depends not just on God, but also upon the courage of the decision of the person within particular moments.[7]

Given the possible choices of value that God provides, each person has to decide how much risk to take. With every decision, there are pressures toward continuity and pressures toward novelty. We have the hard task of trying to prevent the goodness of the past from being destroyed and trampled by the human desire for excitement while supporting the necessary novelty to construct a new future. Chaos and loss of value is a continuous threat. The risk of chaos is the destruction of the stream of occasions that make up the society of which it is part, which humans experience as the threat of death. In this sense, every human being is naturally conservative, desiring to survive and preserve the values that have sustained us so far.

However, the past also includes contradictions that threaten the dream of a new future. Our ancestors faced the challenges of their lives as best they could, but they were not able to do everything. Some of their dreams are yet to be realized. New levels of harmony and qualitative change come only through risk and extended periods of relative chaos, what Christians sometimes call the process of death and resurrection. In the moment of decision, the person cannot know the future. God empowers persons to become and gives us the data we need for our decisions. God lures us toward increased value, but we are free to act with courage or not. Lack of courage is a constant temptation that leads to sin and evil. Sometimes we are terrified of what we are called to do, and we choose to be passive at crucial moments. We avoid risk by doing nothing, tragically allowing the moment of transformation to pass. Sometimes we try to control the future by controlling others. However, abuse of power for control violates the relationality of the created order and leads to heartbreak and loneliness. Only through courageous risk and vulnerability can human beings preserve the best of the past and bring novelty that will fulfill the dreams of humanity for a peaceful and prosperous world.

> Does God change? If not, can humans have real relationships with God? If so, can we count on God to be always loving?

Given this view of God and human nature, process theology understands God and humans as partners in creating value in the processive flow of life. God and humans are not peers because God acts to preserve goodness within creation and the full knowledge of good and evil, and humans do not. But humans make choices that help determine whether the past is preserved and future dreams come to reality. In the ideal world, God and the world, especially humans, work together for good and the world becomes a more beautiful place for all creatures.

HUMAN RELIGIOUS EXPERIENCE

For survivors of sexual and domestic violence, God as Father and Creator is an ambiguous character. One of the favorite narratives of the prevention of domestic violence movement is 2 Samuel 13, the rape of Tamar by her brother, Amnon. While God is not an active character in this story as it is recorded, survivors find comfort that the story of a victim of sexual violence and her courageous witness has been preserved in the Hebrew Bible. Tamar is the hero of the story. At the beginning, she has no way of knowing that her brother, Amnon, and his cousin, Jonadab, have engaged in a conspiracy to entrap her into sexual abuse. They even manipulate her father, King David, into helping by ordering Tamar to visit Amnon on his sickbed. This conspiracy creates a situation where Tamar is alone with Amnon in his bedroom with no protection from violence. When she learns of his intent, she forcefully argues her case: "No, my brother, do not force me; for such a thing is not done in Israel; do not do anything so vile! As for me, where could I carry my shame? And as for you, you would be as one of the scoundrels in Israel. Now therefore, I beg you, speak to the king; for he will not withhold me from you" (2 Sam. 13:12-13). Amnon is not persuaded and he overpowers her and rapes her.

The aftermath of rape reveals the usual male responses of violence against women. Amnon is enraged with her and wants her to disappear; David is worried about the fate of his oldest son, Amnon, and refuses to protect or comfort Tamar; Absalom uses the rape of his sister as an occasion to get revenge and eliminate a rival for his own ambitions to the throne. All three men show cowardice in facing the tragedy that has unfolded in their family.[8]

When survivors read this story, they quickly recognize the human plot—the male conspiracy, the vulnerable but courageous victim, the cowardly father, and the vengeful male relative. Many survivors report that their own experience is a close parallel; for many, there were years of abuse, collusion, silence, and rationalization that heaped trauma upon trauma. The story is empowering for some because they can clearly see Tamar's resistance to evil even though it was not an effective deterrent to victimization. But then they ask theological questions: Where was God during the rape of Tamar? What is God's responsibility for creating a hostile social context in which women are sexualized and made vulnerable by male attitudes and behaviors? Why didn't God intervene in this situation to protect Tamar when God saw her righteousness? Where was God during the aftermath when Tamar disappeared as a disgraced princess? Even though God is not a character in the story, God is a member of the covenant that made Tamar vulnerable to rape. The silence of God in this story often matches the survivors' experience in which she prayed for help and the abuse continued.

There are many other biblical stories of violence against women that are tragic because the victims are never given voice and never heard from again. Examples include Jephthah's daughter (Judges 11), Queen Vashti (Esther 1), and Lot's daughters (Genesis 19). There are also a few stories of justice. For example, in Daniel 13,[9] Susanna is attacked by two corrupt judges in her garden. When she resists and screams, they accuse her of adultery, give witness against her, and she is sentenced to die. In the nick of time, Daniel suspects that the judges are giving false witness. He entraps them in contradictions and vindicates Susanna; the judges are sentenced to death for their false witness. It is one of the few biblical stories of sexual violence where justice is done for the victim.[10]

Survivors ask several important questions to traditional Christian theology about God. Why did God create a world in which some persons are victims of violence at the hands of others? Why is God sometimes silent when the victims of violence cry out in prayer for safety and healing? How does God participate in the healing process that must occur for survivors of violence to construct a full humanity? These are painful questions that drive some survivors away from Christian faith and away from Christian community. Other survivors blame the evil actions on human beings who abuse others and find comfort in their faith. For some, God provides support and comfort during times of abuse. God brings resources in the form of courage and empathic partners that lead to healing. Out of these hard questions comes a new witness about the nature of God.

> Survivors of violence give witness to the absence of God. Is this a problem of human limitation? Is this a problem for a doctrine of God?

From this brief review of Scripture, tradition, and the religious witness of survivors, I come to the following affirmations about God, the first person of the Trinity: God's character is relational, ambiguous, and resilient.

GOD'S RELATIONAL CHARACTER

Study of Scripture, theology, and contemporary witness is arriving at a consensus that God is relational by nature. When God made humans "in God's image," God embedded us in our relationships with one another, the natural world and the earth, and with Godself. That is, we know who we are through our relationships. We are born to parents, raised in families, nurtured in communities, and find work in communities and

institutions with other people. Our life is made up of relationships. Likewise, many current doctrines of the Trinity emphasize the relationality
of the three persons in one Godhead. The Trinity symbolizes a way that
unity and diversity, individuality and community exist in a harmony of
contrasts that does not diminish the uniqueness of any person.[11]

The nature of God's relationality is controversial, however. Even
though every modern theology teaches that God is love and God loves
the world, the meaning of this love is contested. If the nature of God's
transcendence includes the idea that God is unchanging and unchange-
able, then how can there be mutual love between God and humans? If
God does not need human love, and if God is not affected by human
love, not even the fervent prayers of those who seek God, then what
does it mean to say God is love?

In the twenty-first century, we in Western culture have inherited an
individualistic perspective based on ancient and modern philosophy and
theology. Within the metaphysics of Western philosophy a basic distinction is made between being and nonbeing. Being is the ground of all
that exists and never changes; an existing being is a mixture of being and
nonbeing that comes into existence, lives for a time, and dies; that is,
an existing being goes from nonbeing to being and returns to nonbeing.
Therefore, existence is a lesser form than being. Within this theology
God is defined as being itself or the ground of being. God's love sustains
existence in a benevolent way, but God is not affected by existent beings
because God is pure being and does not partake of nonbeing.

What does it mean for a human being to be in a covenant of love
with being itself or the ground of being?[12] Modern theology based in
European existentialism asserts that God loves the world but is unable
to explain the meaning of this love in ways that humans can understand.
God must be unchanging, all-powerful, all-loving, and omniscient, the
characteristics of being within existential philosophy. Because of the
contradictory logic of this combination of characteristics theologians
have spent much energy defending God against the questions about the
existence of evil and the meaning of love (questions of theodicy and the
efficacy of prayer).[13]

Process theology, in contrast to European existential philosophy,
puts change or process at the center of reality. According to Whitehead, change does not mean the loss of being. In fact, existence is the
purpose of God's creativity. Put another way, God is an existent being,

which is possible because Creativity, the ultimate principle of reality, is change itself. Therefore, God can exist and participate in change without ceasing to be God. God and human beings are not equal and the same. That is, human experience exists only momentarily, and what we know as persons are actually enduring societies of many experiences over time. In contrast, God is a changing being who does not exist momentarily, but eternally, and whose function is to offer an initial aim to every human being in its flow of experience. God and actual entities are qualitatively different from one another because their functions in the world are quite different. But God is real and interacts with humans in intimate ways.

God is an active agent in the center of every human life, and the decision of every moment of experience is received into the life of God. God has two functions in the world: one is to promote value through influence in each moment of experience; the other is to receive and preserve each experience as a contribution to the future. God is an agent of love and power in the world, acting to create good and resist evil, saving the world and its values for the future.

Within process theology the mutual influence between God and human beings is asymmetrical. Human beings are decisively shaped by God's influence in their lives because of the crucial role of the initial aim of values. God is shaped by the influence of human beings because God receives the energy from each moment of experience into God's existence. The actual impact upon God of any particular moment of experience is quite small when one considers the billions of experiences in each moment of history. By the transcendent nature of God, process theology means that God transcends the perspective of any human being. God is immanent within each moment of experience, but God transcends each actual moment so totally that there no way that an actual entity can perceive God's perspective on things. It is true that God creates the world in each moment, and it is true that human beings influence God, however infinitesimally.

It makes sense within process theology to say that God and the world are relational and have intersubjective interactions. Human beings are made up of relationships including God, other beings, and the natural world. God's life is constantly influenced by the decisions of human beings and all creation. Thus, within process theology God loves in a way that humans can understand. What happens in my life matters to God, because the relative value I achieve in my life, with God's help, contributes to the value and beauty of the world and God's interior life. If the goal of creation is an increase in value, then the value of my life either contributes to or subtracts from the value of the world and God.

Process theologian Bernard Loomer defines love as the ability to sustain relationships over time with all of their contrasts and contradictions and move those relationships toward harmony and beauty.[14] If love is defined in this way, then to say that God is love means that God sustains a relationship with me through all the ups and downs of my life. What I make of what I have been given contributes to God; it is my gift to God and the world. God and humans have real relationships that can be called loving. God is love, and the call to humans is to love self, others, and God in the same way that God does: "'You shall love the Lord your God with all your heart, and with all your soul, and with all your mind.' This is the greatest and first commandment. And a second is like it: 'You shall love your neighbor as yourself.' On these two commandments hang all the law and the prophets" (Matt. 22:37-40).

Survivors of sexual violence who have experienced healing sometimes witness that there is a relational God in the universe. Even though they suffered evil abuse that nearly broke their spirits and ended their lives, many have also found fragile connections with compassionate others who comforted and sustained them. Linda Crockett writes about the images of a lady in white and a little boy named Peter who

What do we mean when we say "God is love?"

came to her often after sessions of abuse by her mother. She would go to her favorite tree in the nearby woods and be comforted by the lady in white. Her friend Peter would play with her and give his unconditional love. While these figures were spiritual rather than human, they saved her life and enabled her to endure until she found concrete human beings who offered her unconditional love and support. Through many years of healing work, she learned the meaning of love and power and developed a ministry with other survivors of violence. She understands God has a loving spiritual presence in ways that are compatible with the view of process theology.[15] Philip's depression based on personal and social abuses led him to contemplate suicide often and contributed to his desperate attempt to seek intimacy by abusing others. Somehow he endured and yearns for relationships that are mutual, respectful, and intimate. His life is a witness to the reality of God's presence in desperate circumstances.

GOD'S AMBIGUITY

To say that God is radically relational leads to the additional insight that God is ambiguous. At one level, this means that God's morality transcends human understanding so much that human judgments about good and evil are only partially correct in the life of God. But God's ambiguity is more than human ambiguity and inability to conceive of the full reality of God. In process theology, God's ambiguity arises from the fact that every moment is a convergence of the contradictions from the past and hopes for the future. If divine and human decisions lead to an increase in value, then it ushers in a new world with new contradictions. The direction of creativity is toward more complexity—"the many become one and are increased by one," as Whitehead wrote.[16] There is no resting point that is beyond all contradictions—although there are moments of peace and serene beauty when contradictions are overcome to the best extent possible under the circumstances. But the process continues into the next moments when new challenges to harmony arise. What is beautiful in one moment can become mundane and eventually ugly in the next moments as the ignored contradictions become evident.

God's ambiguity means that God and humans strive for "the more," for more harmony, more beauty, more complexity, more power, more love.[17] This striving is built into the process of Creativity itself. However, there is a side of Creativity as process that does not care about value, and is content as long as the process continues, even if it disintegrates into chaos. The role of God is to guide Creativity toward greater harmony and beauty, and this is accomplished through God's covenants with actual moments of experience. The joint project between God and humans can be characterized as love, as mutual covenant. And whether the process leads to the good depends on the ability of God and humans to tolerate ambiguity.

One meaning of ambiguity is that human beings are not single-minded in our daily lives. In his research, Freud noticed a tendency within humans to split reality into rigid categories of good and evil. This process of splitting he judged to be a stage of development in between the stage of perceiving reality as undifferentiated and the stage of perceiving reality with complexity and contradictions. He referred to this latter stage as ambivalence, which he defined as the ability to accept simultaneous subjective feelings of love and hate toward a beloved figure in one's life. Thus, within psychoanalytic psychology, ambivalence or ambiguity is a more mature developmental stage than splitting one's perceptions into categories of good and evil.

Another meaning of ambiguity is that what is good in one moment can become evil in the next. Freud noticed that his patients might make a significant insight at one moment, only to become defensive and rigid again in the future. Thus, psychoanalyst Robert Langs is purported to have said, "Today's insight becomes tomorrow's defense."[18] Loomer refers to the theologian Reinhold Niebuhr, who said the same thing in another way: "[Niebuhr's] insight that every advance in goodness brings with it the possibility of greater evil entails the caveat that there is no progressive conquest of evil. . . . [E]very creative advance may give rise to its contrary or to some condition that either negates or qualifies the advance."[19]

Many survivors of abuse and violence suffer from post-traumatic stress disorder.[20] One of the main characteristics of this disorder is rigid polarization that can mean dramatic changes in personality—from obsession with memories of the abuse to complete dissociation from these memories; from depression and inability to function to times of manic behaviors that are potentially destructive; from fear of relationships to rage and a wish to abuse others; from hatred of sexuality to hypersexual activity. The process of healing inevitably requires a gradual process of reviewing one's history of abuse and working through the range of contradictory feelings and thoughts that dominate one's life. Healing also involves learning both how to trust others and be vulnerable and how to set limits when others try to abuse their power. The end result of healing is an acceptance that all these contradictions are a part of oneself and that one can become strong enough to live with internal ambiguity and ambivalence toward self and others. In this sense, ambiguity is a sign of significant healing and maturity for survivors.[21]

> We know that human life is ambiguous. But can God be ambiguous?

I believe that accepting ambiguity is a sign of maturity for all human beings, and by analogy I believe the same is true for God. God is one who feels the vortex of all of the ambiguities of history and the present moment and engages faithfully in helping to create greater value and multiplicity even when it creates more moral ambiguity. In this sense, acceptance of ambiguity creates the conditions for doing good.

GOD'S RESILIENCE

Human history, including the stories of the Scriptures, indicates that there is no guaranteed progress toward increased value in the world. Every time some gain in value appears, an equally sinister form of evil is possible. David defeated Goliath and became the beloved king. Then he abused his power when he murdered Uriah in order to possess Bathsheba. Israel became a great nation, but abused the poor and vulnerable just as other nations had. The disciples followed Jesus, but they refused to accept his concepts of love and power and abandoned him at his crucifixion. Jesus was raised from the dead and the Spirit was sent to the new church. But soon the churches were fighting with one another for power and control. Constantine was converted to Christianity, ending the persecution of Christians. But he coerced the baptism of all Roman subjects and killed those who refused to submit to his power. Human history is a tragic story of achievement of value followed by new forms of corruption and abuse of power. Modern science in Christian nations has ushered in amazing advances in human health and productivity side by side with the most horrendous violence in human history.

Is God resilient? This is what the psalmists wanted to know, and what survivors of abuse want to know. Does God remain faithful to the covenant with the poor and vulnerable during and after a reign of evil? Does God side with the powerful against the vulnerable, or does God hear the cries of the poor and sustain the covenant for a new day of justice and recreation? Does God have the power to absorb the tragedy of human and natural life and sustain the value of creation and history for the future?

In my work with survivors, many report that they felt the absence and silence of God and felt abandoned at times of vulnerability. They want to know: Is this abandonment permanent? Or does God return for a new day of empowerment and loving relationship? In clinical terms, is there healing for one's spirit after the trauma of violence? Is there any community where I can be accepted? Does God answer my prayers anymore?

I believe the answer to this question is that God's love and power are resilient. Some survivors report that when they cry to God, their prayers are answered. There may be long periods of silence when God seems to be absent. But God's Spirit will not be squelched forever. Eventually God returns.

Within my theology, the risk of a fully relational, ambiguous God is that the conspiracy of human evil can eclipse God for a season. This is the only way I can explain the witness of some survivors who have endured decades of trauma without relief. Human freedom to choose evil combined with institutions and ideologies of evil over generations create conditions that cannot be quickly altered. The results of evil are always tragic, a permanent loss of value and life. Evil effects are long lasting; no future value can justify the losses from a reign of evil.

There is genuine evil when human lives are lost, human spirits are crushed, and the creation itself is irrevocably damaged. In these situations, the resilience of God means that God continues to act for the good and remembers those who are lost; God does not forget the heroism of those who resisted evil. For those who survive evil, God is resilient. God provides new resources for healing, hope, and empowerment. During the healing process, survivors give witness of the hidden ways that God was present in the midst of the trauma. There seems to be no limit to hope when the resilience of human beings and the resilience of God come together. I have seen miracles that could not be explained. Where does a survivor's resilience come from? It is the combination of her own resilience as a human being and the resilience of God. In a world where evil is real and lasting, there is nothing that can destroy the resilience of God and the resilience of the human spirit. This is the meaning of Romans 8:38-39: "For I am convinced that neither death, nor life, nor angels, nor rulers, nor things present, nor things to come, nor powers, nor height, nor depth, nor anything else in all creation, will be able to separate us from the love of God in Christ Jesus our Lord."

Within process theology, God's ontological function of providing an initial aim for every occasion and unfailingly receiving the free decisions of all occasions is a sign of resilience. The existence of the world depends on God's everlasting response within the concreteness of each moment. God's initial aim is a powerful influence toward more value for each occasion; but whether such value is actualized depends on the courage within each momentary occasion. It is possible within such a cosmology for occasions and systems of occasions to become organized in an evil direction that is destructive of harmonious community. God's influence toward value is not always sufficient to counter the momentum of such evil systems in their ascendancy. However, God continues to act with power toward concrete occasions and greater value. As evil begins the inevitable self-destructive phase of its life cycle, God is present to preserve what value can be preserved, to support the resistance and creativity of prophetic actions, and to call all persons toward greater value. This view of God confirms the religious experience of survivors of violence about God's resilience.

For example, one of my male clients was sexually abused and traumatized as a child; he coped the best he could, but when he had opportunity as a parent, he became an abuser who did the same things that had created the trauma in his own life to a child in his care. The absence of God in his life seemed to contribute to the passing of evil from one generation to another. I think of sexually trafficked women who survive decades of forced prostitution, and then later become madams enforcing sexual slavery on other children similar to what they themselves had experienced. Where is the love of God in such a story? I believe that we must allow for the felt absence of God's love in particular moments of radical evil. But we can continue to believe in the resilience of God's love. That is, God's love can be rejected in particular circumstances by human decisions, but God's love is resilient and will return again and again.

> Are God's love and power everlasting? Where are God's love and power during the reigns of terror that humans create?

The Christian mythos about the resilience of God is the death and resurrection of Jesus Christ. God did not prevent Jesus' death at the hands of violent religious and political leaders. Some traditions ritualize this moment by extinguishing all the lights in the church in worship on the evening of Good Friday. But God's Spirit was not vanquished by this tragedy. Jesus survived and returned to inspire his disciples. His presence continues to inspire believers in the midst of the most horrendous evils of our time. God's love and power are not destroyed by human sin and evil; God's love and power are resilient.

SUMMARY

I believe in a God who is relational, ambiguous, and resilient. Through the witness of Scripture, process theology, and survivors of violence, I see a God who created the world out of love and lives in covenant with human beings no matter what happens. I see a God who influences every moment of our human experience, and is influenced by the values that humans create through our courageous actions. I see a God who is larger than the valuations of good and evil that we understand and lives with us in the ambiguity of human life. I see a God who never gives up and whose healing power is resilient and everlasting. This is God, the first person of the divine Trinity, who was revealed in Scripture and the life of Jesus Christ, and who continues to act in the lives of people today.

TWO

The Reality
of Evil and Sin

*Human beings are made in the image of God as loving and powerful.
God calls humanity to exercise power in loving ways to advance the
creative purposes of God. However, the history of human life shows
that humans distort the image of God in their hearts and create institutions and ideologies that promote destruction of bodies, persons, and
the ecology of the earth. Human sin becomes systemic evil that leads to
abuse of power, violence, and the destruction of war and environmental catastrophe. Systemic evil promotes individual sin through apathy,
sloth, greed, and other deadly sins. The problem of evil leads to the
question of salvation: What cooperative work of God and humans
will rescue the world from self-destruction and the loss of meaning,
value, and beauty?*

Process theologian Daniel Day Williams has stated clearly the basic for-
mulation of Christian theology: "[Humans] bear the image of God who
is love. [Human] love falls into disorder; but there is a work of God
which restores [human] integrity and power to enter into communion.
Every Christian theology is an elaboration of this theme."[1]

The intentions of God discussed in Chapter 1 are challenged by the
reality of evil. That is, God desires an increase in harmony and beauty
through greater love and power. But tragedy based in accumulated
human decisions for evil frustrates the intentions of God. In the previous
chapter, I discussed the relationality, ambiguity, and resilience of God.
Much of that discussion depended on a theology about God's intentions
and an understanding of human evil. In this chapter I develop a more
systematic discussion of human evil and its characteristics by looking at
Scriptures about evil, process theological reflections about evil, and witness to the reality of evil among survivors of violence.

EVIL AND THE BIBLE

In the Scriptures, God frequently poses a version of this question: "I blessed you and made you prosperous. Yet you turned away from me and followed after other gods. What am I going to do with you?" God seems to waver between destroying the people of Israel and loving them until they change. In the flood story in Genesis 6:13 God says to Noah, "I have determined to make an end of all flesh, for the earth is filled with violence because of them; now I am going to destroy them along with the earth." The prophets name Israel's sins in detail and tell the people that these sins will lead to great punishments. The destruction of the Temple and the captivity of the people in Babylon seem to express the wrathful God who brings punishment for evil and destruction of human bodies and spirits.

Yet there are many Scriptures that speak of the love of God, the agony for God of human sin, and the mercy that God shows toward the people of God, even in the midst of their sin, such as this from Hosea 11:8-9:

> How can I give you up, Ephraim?
>   How can I hand you over, O Israel?
> How can I make you like Admah?
>   How can I treat you like Zeboiim?
> My heart recoils within me;
>   my compassion grows warm and tender.
> I will not execute my fierce anger;
>   I will not again destroy Ephraim;
> for I am God and no mortal,
>   the Holy One in your midst,
>   and I will not come in wrath.

In the Hebrew Scriptures, human sin is a violation of the covenant between God and Israel. Sometimes this is interpreted as disobedience to the laws that defined the covenant. But humans are clever enough to interpret the laws so that they favor the powerful over those with less power. Many of the prophets interpreted sin as a violation of love, the spirit of the law, which is captured in what we call the Golden Rule "You shall not take vengeance or bear a grudge against any of your people, but you shall love your neighbor as yourself: I am the LORD" (Lev. 19:18). Jesus said in Matthew 7:12, "In everything do to others as you would have them do to you; for this is the law and the prophets." These two principles, "Do no harm" (nonmaleficence) and "do good to others" (beneficence)[2] are affirmed in many world religions and philosophies from as early as Hippocrates, Moses, and Confucius.[3]

The Hebrew prophets complained frequently about abuse of power and the mistreatment of those who were vulnerable because of their social status (widows, orphans, and strangers). The nomadic code of hospitality promoted nonviolence and benevolent hospitality toward those who had no home and no social protection because of tragic circumstances and oppression: "For the LORD your God is God of gods and Lord of lords, the great God, mighty and awesome, who is not partial and takes no bribe, who executes justice for the orphan and the widow, and who loves the strangers, providing them with food and clothing. You shall also love the stranger, for you were strangers in the land of Egypt" (Deut. 10:17-19). In the Hebrew Scriptures we can understand human sin and evil as the abuse of power that is destructive of vulnerable persons. The prophets called Israel to repent and return to the covenant with God by doing justice and promoting love.

Jesus' teachings were consistent reaffirmations of the prophetic witness. In the Sermon on the Mount (Matthew 5–7), considered by Anabaptist and Pietist theologians as the canon within the canon, Jesus blessed those who are merciful, the peacemakers, those who are persecuted for righteousness, those who are poor, the meek, those who mourn, and the pure in heart. Jesus said that he had come to fulfill the law, not destroy it. He emphasized the importance of human motivation as well as behavior. You should not murder *and* you should not hate; you should not commit adultery *and* you should not nurture lust; you should not swear falsely *and* you should not swear at all, because everything you say should be the truth; you should not exceed the law of the talon (eye for eye, tooth for tooth) *and* you should not resist evil, but return love for evil; you should love your neighbor as yourself *and* you should love your enemies. From such verses, the Anabaptist-Pietist traditions get the foundation for pacifism, often interpreted as nonviolence or nonviolent resistance to evil.

The central stories that promote a loving use of power are the Passion narratives. Jesus did not defend himself in the garden of Gethsemane, but healed the ear of the guard injured by Peter. Jesus did not defend his prophetic actions in the court with the Sanhedrin or Pilate. He did not resist the mob that called for his crucifixion, or the guards who put him on the cross. Even in the worst of circumstances, Jesus did not resort to violence, even though he said: "Do you think that I cannot appeal to my Father, and he will at once send me more than twelve legions of angels?" (Matt. 26:53).

PROCESS THEOLOGY

In process theology, power is a central concept. Our experiences are created by the power of our relationships from the past, and we exercise power when we pass our life on to others in the future. As each moment of experience comes into being, we feel the impact of the past, the power of others before us that have passed their life on with its mixture of beauty and ugliness, good and evil, complexity and ambiguity. In each moment of experience we feel the powerful impact of the past actual world. We are given a world within which we must "live and move and have our being" (Acts 17:28). God is part of this world because God has influenced each moment of the past, and God has initiated the moments of our own brief existence. Our life is the result of the exercise of power by God and others. Our existence within the world can be described by Bernard Loomer's term, "relational power,"[4] or what I have described as "sensitivity, the ability to feel the feelings of others."[5] This sensitivity is sometimes called "receptive power" because it involves receiving the influence of others. In psychology, empathy involves hearing and understanding the perspective of another person. The practice of empathy is often quite powerful in its effects because people need to be understood, to belong, and to see that their life makes a difference to others.

During the moments of our own internal processes and decision making, we depend on power. Our ability to receive the past and consider alternative responses to the contrasts and contradictions we have received is a form of internal power. Through disciplines of receptivity and thought, we have the option of creative freedom. We are bound to receive the impact of others because we are embedded in our relationships and have no option but to respond to them. We are not totally bound because we have the possibility of responding in unexpected ways. During the moment of consideration of our options, we are exercising the power of individual freedom.

Our momentary existence leads to a point of decision when we pass our life on to others. This response is characterized by power, which means that others have no choice but to receive what we have given to them. Here we have creative power, the power to affect others in ways that they cannot completely ignore. "Human experience is a process of interaction characterized by sensitivity, i.e., feeling the feelings of others, and by creativity, i.e., responding to others with new feelings."[6]

Sometimes power over others is the way the world understands all power. Loomer has called this "unilateral power," the ability to influence others without being influenced by them.[7] Within process theology, however, the power to receive the influence of others, the power to exercise freedom in our private deliberations, and the power to influence others are all part of being human. If we follow the witness from the Scriptures, all of these forms of power should be exercised in love, what I have called loving sensitivity and loving creativity: "Love in human experience is a quality of interaction characterized by sensitivity which moves toward communion with self, others, and God, and by creativity which moves toward enlarged freedom for self, others, and God."[8]

Whether we are receiving from others, reflecting within the interior life of our own spirit, or influencing others, we should be exercising love—the intent and action to increase the communion and freedom of self, others, and God. Sometimes this is called the common good, that is, what would be beneficial for each actual moment and what would be good for the whole society and world of which we are a part. In all this, we hope to respond in love to God who can use our responses to benefit the whole creation.

SIN AND EVIL

Sin is the denial of loving sensitivity, the turning away from communion with self, others, and God. Sin is the willful decision of the individual to value down the relational aspects of life with its consequences of smaller size for all individuals and the totality of the world. . . .

> Sin is the denial of loving creativity, the rejection of enlarged freedom for
> self, others, and God. Sin is the willful decision of an individual to value down
> the freedom of life with its consequences of smaller size for all individuals and
> God.[9]

Human evil arises in the human heart as the refusal to accept power
from others and the refusal to respond with loving creativity to others.
This is abuse of receptive power, the refusal to receive the world that
we have received. Human evil further arises in the human heart as the
refusal to create enlarged freedom for future occasions. This is abuse of
creative power.

However, human evil goes beyond what happens within the individual moment of receptivity, reflection, and creative response because
actual occasions over time create enduring societies with certain characteristics that have long-term influence.

I have defined evil in the following way:

> Genuine evil is the abuse of power destructive to bodies and spirits; Evil is pro-
> duced by personal actions and intentions which are denied and dissociated by
> individuals; evil is organized by economic forces, institutions and ideologies,
> but mystified by appeals to necessity and truth; evil is sanctioned by religion,
> but masked by claims to virtue, love, and justice.[10]

A pattern of sinful decisions eventually creates institutions and
ideologies that are enduring patterns of influence. Thus, human evil
assumes a pattern that cannot be easily changed by individual decisions.

Resistance to evil requires concerted effort by many occasions over
a significant period of time. Construction of genuine good requires a
pattern of disciplined cooperative actions based on an alternative vision
and courageous individuals who often have to suffer for their vision
of the future.

What is your own definition
of genuine evil? How does
human sin contribute to
genuine evil?

We can understand the life,
teachings, and death of Jesus in
terms of resistance to evil and constructive actions to actualize alter-
native forms of human and natural life. The changes that he called for
required the sacrificial commitment of whole communities over generations. His teachings in themselves were not sufficient because the

change he sought was complex. He called for total repentance and new life. When the powers of violence organized themselves against Jesus, the crowds who loved him and the disciples who lived with him were terrified and fled into anonymous security. For many Christians, the crucifixion represents the kind of commitment and sacrifice that sometimes comes to those who love God. If someone as loving and powerful as Jesus could promote his vision of a nonviolent life only by going to the cross, then some of us may also be called to follow him to a cross as we resist the evil of our time. It is not sacrifice and suffering that brings an end to evil, however, but intergenerational resistance and prophetic witness over long periods of time.[11]

WITNESS OF SURVIVORS

Survivors of sexual and domestic violence give vivid witness to the reality of evil and the resilience of divine and human spirits in the face of evil. Survivors of child sexual abuse, for example, who live and find the courage to tell their stories, instruct us on the profundity of evil. First, they have been victims of destructive acts of individuals. At a time of physical and emotional vulnerability, they were coerced into behaviors to satisfy the sexual and power needs of adults without their understanding and consent. Child sexual abuse requires individual agency by abusers. Such acts most often occur in secrecy without the full knowledge of others, although some victims have experienced ritual abuse by groups of adults. In either case, the acts are hidden from the general view of the larger public because they are illegal and abhorrent in nearly every society.

The secrecy of such acts could indicate that child sexual abuse is only an individual sin, and if the secret is told, then justice will be done. We can be thankful that this happens in some circumstances. In many instances, however, silence and collusion by family members and the larger society protects the abuser, especially if that person has social status and respect. If the abuser is an important member of the family, then a charge of sexual abuse by one of the children is sometimes unwelcome. Disclosure leads to disruption and potentially destroys the unity of the family itself. Often the family will engage in various forms of denial and silencing, hoping that their family privacy will remain intact and the charges will go away. When this happens, we see the existence of human evil at the level of the family. First, we see human sin organized at the level of the personality of the abuser; second, we see human sin organized at the level of the family. The ability of the family to enforce silence about child sexual abuse depends on the complicity of the larger society. This often occurs through ideologies about family privacy and parental authority in Western societies. The larger community, including the state in many societies, cannot intervene within the family without cause. The ideologies in some societies consider the family a place where individuals are protected from the state, and where parents are ultimately responsible for the education and welfare of their children. If the family is able to enforce silence about the existence of child sexual abuse, the ideologies of family privacy and parental authority will be sufficient to keep the larger community at bay.

Within and beyond ideologies about the family are ideologies of gender, race, social class, and ableness (normative ideas of what it means to be able-bodied). Therefore, if the victim of child sexual abuse is female, nonwhite, poor, and/or a person with a disability, that victim will be more vulnerable and her complaints more likely to be ignored. For example, a young child with a serious developmental disorder may not be able to communicate her experience effectively, and she may not have the kinds of relationships and communication connections to alert others to what is happening. Human sin leads to pervasive ideologies about what it means to be a valuable, normal human being within a particular society. If persons do not fit into these norms, their experiences are not taken as seriously and their suffering is more likely to be tolerated and ignored.

Within and beyond all of these levels is the level of religious sanction. Every great human evil that persists over time has religious sanction. That means that major religious institutions, leaders, and theologies have promoted ideas that give privilege to certain people in a society and oppress others. In the case of child sexual abuse within the United States, parents are given authority over children, men over women, whites over nonwhites, abled persons over persons who have disabilities, more educated over less educated, rich over poor and working class, and so forth. For example, the long-time teaching of the church about female persons as more sexualized, less moral, less intelligent, and properly subordinate to men at home and in society has created a class of vulnerable persons, namely, female children and adults.[12] When we add to this the repression of healthy sexuality by Western Christianity, then we have a volatile and dangerous contradiction within society that has led to generations of child sexual abuse.

This brief discussion may suffice to see the relationship between individual human sin and the organization of human evil in institutions, ideologies, and religious sanction. How does one begin to understand and change such a system? Evil such as child sexual abuse is a pervasive system with power to influence the future in multiple ways. The alternatives to systemic evil are sustained, organized movements of resistance and creative response over generations. Paul Kivel has advocated what he calls the Fifth Generation Movement, a sustained effort over five generations that could possibly end child sexual abuse. This painful truth is recognition by the sexual and domestic violence movement that the changes we seek to prevent this form of human evil are so deeply embedded in U.S. society that we have to plan for a long and sustained effort to get the changes we want.[13]

This attitude of resistance and long-term change in individuals, institutions, ideologies, and religions was part of Jesus' thinking at the end of his active ministry. He had done what he could through miracles, healings, and teaching and had generated such dedicated opposition to his work that he chose to accept the crucifixion because it was the only way to communicate clearly God's love for humanity. Thousands of years later, people continue to be inspired by his courageous actions, and the deeper meanings of his life, death, and resurrection continue to be rescued from the religious authorities who want to control Jesus' memory for themselves.[14]

> What are the human motives for sin and evil?

MOTIVES FOR DOING EVIL

We have discussed the forms of human sin and evil. But what is the motive for doing evil? What do humans hope to accomplish by turning away from the goodness of communion and freedom God calls us

to enjoy? Daniel Day Williams has written one of the most inspired
answers to these questions:

> We are created for communion with God and our neighbor in a life which
> offers communion on terms which require courage and trust in a future we
> cannot see, which postpones fulfillment and does not allow every kind of
> immediate gratification. When we discover the risks involved in being human
> in the great community we are anxious, and when we do not find the hope of
> communion we are desperate. We willingly deny the fullness of our humanity
> in order to gratify some part of it. We choose to be human on terms which are
> immediately satisfying, self-protective, and comfortable. But this choice can
> be an act of self-destruction, and in the depths of our being we know it. Like
> Albert Camus' Jean Baptiste in *The Fall*, we have refused to respond to the cry
> of another human being, and we are now less than the persons we must be if
> we are to accept life.
>
> It is not a long step in the logic of emotions to will to destroy the sensitiv-
> ity of life itself, to turn against ourselves and everything which symbolizes full
> humanity. We kill what we love because we refuse to love on the terms which
> life gives. Hannah Arendt speaks in her study of the Eichmann trial of the
> 'banality' of evil. The secret of that banality is here. Human evil is in some
> sense a rejection of life, that is, a rejection of what makes us truly human
> beings. To be human is to search for the terms on which the self can be itself in
> relation to every other self.[15]

These paragraphs summarize my thinking about the motive for
human evil. I have seen this reality in my work with men who have
sexually abused children. The abusive men I have known well came
from emotionally impoverished backgrounds where human kindness
and support during childhood was absent or unreliable. In some cases
the person who related to them with the most warmth and support was
the same person who sexually abused them. In this setting, they saw the
world as a place where communion and freedom were rare events that
could not provide the basis for their own hopes and fears. The result
was a life of emptiness, depression, and manipulation to get what they
needed in life. Often their interior barrenness was matched by empty
marriages, dead-end jobs, and lack of real relationships with extended
family and peers.

Sometimes these men were able to manage for years without engaging in destructive behaviors. But in a moment of crisis, when they felt

overwhelmed with despair, they turned to abuse in order to obtain something for themselves. As Williams says, they became desperate when they could not find the hope of communion and freedom. In response to this internal crisis they created a fantasy about who they were, what they needed, and devised multiple rationalizations for what they were about to do. They sexualized their needs for communion and sought pleasure and pseudo-intimacy where they could find it. Often their crisis corresponded with access to a vulnerable child and they convinced themselves that their behaviors would not be harmful to the child. They often found a kind of support for their delusions in certain social attitudes toward sexuality and children. Over time they engaged in grooming behaviors designed to flatter the child and overcome her or his inner resistance, or to frighten the child into cooperation and silence.

"*We willingly deny the fullness of our humanity in order to gratify some part of it. We choose to be human on terms which are immediately satisfying, self-protective, and comfortable.*" They engaged in the sexual abuse of a child; the excitement of the hunt masked their depression. While they may have had pangs of remorse afterward, their need for pseudo-intimacy became strong again, and their rationalizations developed another layer of legitimacy in their minds. They repeat the behaviors over time until there was little internal resistance left.

"*It is not a long step in the logic of emotions to will to destroy the sensitivity of life itself, to turn against ourselves and everything which symbolizes full humanity.*" Eventually they became hardened to the injury they cause, and their rationalizations seemed unassailable. They refused to see that their behaviors were destroying communion and freedom not only for themselves, but also for the child, for the extended family, and for the larger society. They accepted the most horrendous evil, destroying the internal life of a child for short-term falsified gratification. They turned away from the sensitivity of life itself and turned themselves into monsters in the life of the child.

Society bears responsibility for creating institutions and ideologies that rationalize certain forms of evil. In many cases, society refuses to believe that any adult would molest a child. The ideologies of society often silence the child and make her afraid to describe her suffering. Some sex offenders are exposed for their evil deeds, and the larger society transforms them into monsters to face a lifetime of stigma. Society scapegoats some sex offenders because it does not want to examine its own complicity in the ideological distortions of human sexuality, gender, childhood, race, class, and other forms of oppression.

"We kill what we love because we refuse to love on the terms which life gives." Child sexual abuse is a destructive act because of the lifetime of damage it does to someone who has not yet had a chance to live. We know from the witness of adult survivors what some of these consequences are. Some have referred to child abuse as a form of "soul murder"[16] because of the depth of injury that occurs. I know from engaging in psychotherapy with abusers that there is a kind of self-destructive process at work in the life of the abuser as well. Abusers have turned away from real life and have substituted a fantasy that distracts the empty self from its despair. In the process their true self is dying from lack of real relationships. Abusers withdraw from other adult relationships in order to feed their obsession and control the dangers surrounding them.

For the abuser, the sexual abuse of a child creates a delusion about self, other, and the world that alternates between control and chaos. The excitement of maintaining the secret becomes an addiction. As the danger escalates and the contradictions mount, it is possible to understand the murder of a child. I recently talked with a pastor of a church where a faithful church member had killed his young daughter in raging despair as the only way he could see to stop the sexual abuse he was perpetrating on her. He blamed her for causing his fall into evil, and killed her in the mistaken notion that this act would destroy the evil in himself. Murder and suicide are the logical outcome of child sexual abuse. Every survivor I have talked to has said that she feared at some point that she would be killed by her abuser. Rape, murder, and suicide are not uncommon in our society. Many survived serious physical injury when the abuser expressed his rage against her.

All the abusers who stayed in psychotherapy for years confessed that the despair in their lives was always nearby, threatening to engulf them. Alternately they were suicidal and in a manic state about their lives. And when the truth was disclosed and there was no way to lie their way out of trouble, they felt a sense of relief. The truth, as horrible as it was, was preferable to living in a world of death and despair. None of my clients could sustain their commitment to truth consistently, but if therapy progressed, they touched on the truth more and more often until it slowly became preferable to the world of lies they had created.

Many abusers were furious with the larger society for giving them mixed messages about what was possible. While they knew the taboos about sexually exploiting children, they also watched the sexualization of children and the misogyny toward women in the media. In a sense they were living out the repressed shadow of the larger society and knew it. To the extent that they had become attached to the child they abused, they sometimes felt remorse for the consequences in her life. These are the first signs that the resilient God of love and power is active even in the life of a child molester and that healing and restoration of humanity is possible even for these despised ones.

> Can I understand the temptations toward evil in child abusers? Can I identity the temptations toward evil in myself?

SUMMARY

Humans are created for communion and enlarged freedom within a world of relationships. Life is an adventure[17] because the process of creativity as guided by God's love and power is a constant source of wonder and intrigue. As we live within the world of bodies and spirits in relationships, our energy can be directed toward creating new value. The lure of beauty is endlessly fascinating.

But the world as it exists also contains risks that lead to human anxiety and fear. As we become aware of these risks, we are tempted to turn against the flow of brute reality and seek safety and control within a smaller, manageable world. However, by making the decision to turn away from the relational matrix of the empirical world we live in and creating a fantasy that we think will be more pleasant, we actually engage in human sin and contribute to the already existing world of human evil in the form of institutions, ideologies, and religions. When we take the first step in this direction, we enter a slippery slope that leads to death. We can never be sure if or when we will wake from our fantasy and be willing to return to reality again. Sin and evil lead to death, the denial of the sensitivity and creativity that God has given us as a gift. As Paul wrote,

For I do not do the good I want, but the evil I do not want is what I do. Now if I do what I do not want, it is no longer I that do it, but sin that dwells within me. So I find it to be a law that when I want to do what is good, evil lies close at hand. For I delight in the law of God in my inmost self, but I see in my members another law at war with the law of my mind, making me captive to the law of sin that dwells in my members. Wretched man that I am! Who will rescue me from this body of death? Thanks be to God through Jesus Christ our Lord! (Rom. 7:19-25)

THREE
Christology and the Question of Salvation

The problem of evil leads to the question of salvation: What cooperative work of God and humans will rescue the world from self-destruction and the loss of meaning, value, and beauty?

The plot of the Christian narrative I am describing is this: God's intentions for humanity and the world are good, but these intentions are thwarted by human sin that has evolved into evil embedded in institutions, ideologies, and religions. Non-Christian religions have some version of this plot—that the original goodness of creation has been negatively affected by human ignorance or sin. The heart of several religions is an attempt to discover the human response that will restore the intention of the gods and lead to increased value in the world and beyond. Within each religion, there are a variety of responses to the state of the world that span a continuum from withdrawal or escape from the world to intense activism to save the world.

Jesus was from Galilee, one of the poorest areas of Israel, the breadbasket for both temple and empire (Matt. 3:13; 21:11). The peasants of Galilee had been forced off their land through taxes and indebtedness and had become day workers on land their families used to own. Jesus was often mistaken for a Zealot because he championed the cause of the peasants and challenged the oppressive religious and political systems. Many of Jesus' teachings gave voice to the complaints from Galilee about economic oppression and corruption at the highest levels. Jesus was apparently one of hundreds of such local leaders and teachers who were trying to cope with the terror and oppression of the time.

According to the writings about Jesus in the Christian canon, Jesus had unusual abilities to inspire and impress the "people of the land."[1]

He provided food for those who lived in poverty; he healed the sick and mentally ill; he taught large crowds about the love of God and the power of prayer; he challenged the religious leaders to be faithful to their tradition and end the accommodation to empire and accumulation of wealth; he gathered disciples and taught them theology and ministry practices. His ministry began in the countryside and gradually moved toward Jerusalem, the location of the Temple and the center of religious and political power. For the most part the Jesus movement was a typical reform movement like many others before and since. Jesus identified with the most vulnerable people and organized them so that he could challenge the oppression from Jerusalem and Rome. He called for forgiveness of the sin and the indebtedness of the poor that was created by the religious and economic laws of the time. He called the people to follow him even if it required risk and suffering. He taught the disciples how to be grassroots leaders with a vision for change.

However, the Jesus' movement was cut short when he was arrested, tortured, tried, convicted, and crucified for sedition and blasphemy. The people who believed in him felt betrayed when they saw his apparent failure. The disciples ran away in terror and denied that they ever knew Jesus. The religious and political leaders felt justified in their actions and moved on to other challenges to their authority. Apparently, thousands of would-be reformers in Palestine were crucified and killed during the tense years of the first century C.E.

After Pentecost, the disciples claimed that Jesus was resurrected from the dead after three days and they organized to continue their movement for reform and religious revival. Rome's oppression of Palestine continued, however, and when a Zealots' revolt took over the Temple in 68 C.E., Rome sent in a large military force and killed many people living in Israel, dispersing tens of thousands of Jews over the known world. This was the end of the Temple-centered Jewish religion in Israel. Much of the Christian New Testament was written and edited after 70 C.E. with full knowledge of the Roman persecution of the Jews and extension of the Jewish Diaspora.

Many Christians believe that the life, death, and resurrection of Jesus have universal significance that forever changed the relationship of God and humanity. Because of Jesus' incarnation and resurrection, God and humanity have been reconciled; evil and death have been overcome. Through faith it is now possible for humans to live in communion with

God. Christian theology is the effort to restate the narratives about Jesus into doctrines and practices that can sustain communities of believers in new situations. Systematic theology started when Paul wrote letters to the struggling churches of the first century C.E. and continues whenever Christians gather to worship and confess their faith in Christ.

THE QUESTION OF CHRISTOLOGY

The question of the meaning of Jesus Christ within Christianity is called Christology. Unsurprisingly, there is a huge debate among Christians about what happened and what changed in the divine-human relationship because of Jesus, what happened in his life, death, and resurrection that is salvific, and what kind of faith and practices are appropriate for faithful Christians. In this chapter I briefly review some contemporary arguments about Christology and in the following chapter I turn to my own constructive response.

> What changed in the divine-human relationship because of Jesus?

The practices of Christianity today create a huge tent with many possibilities for answering the question of Christology. Within the United States Christianity can be understood as a continuum with two poles. At one pole are those who believe that following Jesus in faith requires social activism to create God's intentions within history. The result is active commitment to individual and social transformation and justice. At the other pole are those who believe that following Jesus requires individual repentance and conversion to faith in Jesus, which will lead to eternal life in heaven after death. Acting for social justice is sometimes appropriate, but the real work of Christians is evangelism—the rescue and conversion of individuals so they will be saved after death and after the end of history, which could come at any time. The basic conflict between these two poles is whether faith in Jesus means saving individuals from history or transforming history into the kingdom of God. Many U.S. Christians would put themselves in between, believing in reforms in history but also believing in individual salvation and eternal life after death. Many Christians in local communities believe what they are taught in the churches—if not with enthusiasm, at least "just in case"[2]—which means, it is best to believe both myths just in case one or both are true.

Much of the debate about the transformation that took place in Jesus Christ centers on the cross. Why did Jesus die, and what did his death accomplish in the life of God and/or human history? I rely on contemporary feminist theologians who focus especially on the problem of violence against women. I will not review all of the viable forms of Christology in the United States, let alone all the options across the many cultures where there are Christian churches. Rather, I review some of the options that have had a particular impact on my own religious imagination and faith.

For many U.S. Christians today the cross is a symbol of God's love for humanity, and a model of self-sacrifice that Christian love requires. When they join in the Eucharist, many believers are reminded that God's loving presence is with them, and they are inspired to express the same kind of love to one another and especially to those who are oppressed and marginalized in our modern society. For other Christians, the cross is a symbol of personal salvation available because of Jesus' sacrifice and the resurrection is a symbol of God's victory over sin and death creating a path for eternal life. For most Christians today, Christianity without the cross is unthinkable.

Theologies of atonement are one attempt to answer the question about the meaning of the cross. Some Christians prefer Anselm's theory of substitutionary atonement, that Jesus' death satisfied the legal penalty for sin and rescued individuals from the penalty of eternal damnation and afterlife in hell. Other Christians prefer Abelard's moral influence theory, that Jesus provided a path to righteousness through sacrificial love which empowers human beings to follow Jesus and bring justice in the world. Irenaeus's ransom (or *Christus Victor*) theory is also influential. In this theory, the reign of God was disrupted by the lies of Satan. God sent Jesus to free the world from the power of Satan, and Jesus' death on the cross was a ransom to the devil that frees human beings and empowers them for righteousness. This latter theory is sometimes attractive to liberation or revolution theologians.[3]

WITNESS OF SURVIVORS OF VIOLENCE

Survivors in the movement to prevent domestic violence have several complaints about the cross as a symbol for Christian faith. Many of these complaints are based on the actual advice survivors received from pastors as they sought support in the midst of violence, including these examples:

1. "It's your cross. You have to bear it like Jesus did." If we are disciples of Christ, then we should follow in Jesus' steps. Just as he went to the cross without complaint and gave his life in obedience to God, so should Christians today be willing to suffer and die, even if that death comes at the hand of one's husband. Survivors object because they refuse to accept any justification for their suffering.

> Is partner battering a form of "persecution for righteousness' sake?"

2. "You must forgive your husband, like Jesus forgave his persecutors on the cross. If Jesus forgave his enemies while he was being killed, we should be able to forgive for much lesser offenses." "You should forgive your husband seventy seven times a day if necessary because that is the way Jesus taught." Survivors object because forgiving abusers keeps them trapped in violent relationships.

3. "The woman is called to obey and submit to her husband and family, just as Jesus showed obedience and submission to God when he went to the cross. Rather than resist his fate, he turned his life over to God—'Not my will, but Thine be done.' In this prayer, Jesus revealed that obedience to God is the pathway to salvation. The pathway for women is obedience to their husbands as Christ was obedient to God the Father." Survivors object because submitting to their husbands often leads to more violence.

> Are Christians required to forgive those who abuse them?

4. "Your suffering is righteous, like Jesus' suffering on the cross. Your husband may be moved by your suffering and saved through your faith. Since Jesus suffered on the cross and died, we should not complain about our suffering, especially if our suffering is innocent like that of Jesus. Suffering is an important part of Christian life: God is trying to teach us something, or God is using us to help someone else. If we die in a righteous

> Are Christian women commanded to submit to their husband's authority?

cause, we are being faithful to God in Jesus Christ and our suffering can be
a road to salvation for ourselves and others." Survivors object because suffering itself is not redemptive unless justice follows. Many battered women
are killed in domestic violence and no good comes from it.

Survivors have objected to these and other misuses of the cross.
Many pastors have encouraged passivity in the face of violence and
maintenance of male domination and injustice. As feminist theologian
Marit Trelstad writes, "[The cross]
supports systems of oppression by
demanding self-sacrifice and suffering from the weak while at the same
time justifying or, worse, sanctifying
oppression and abuse by the power-

**Is suffering a sign of Chris-
tian discipleship?**

ful."[4] In our context, survivors have been encouraged to be sacrificial and
long suffering while perpetrators have been quickly forgiven and restored
to community.

Survivors of violence have complained about such bad theology. One
example of such a complaint is the following poem by Lutheran chaplain
Larraine Frampton, written in the 1980s and published in 1992.

In the name of the Father of and of the Son
And of the Holy Spirit, Amen.

Our Father who art in heaven,
Hallowed be Thy name . . .

Faith of our father's living still . . .
Of the Father's love begotten.

Liturgical melodies weave in and out
Causing patriarchy to be sacred.

Unspoken, unlabeled actions go sin free,
While the guiltless continue their confessions.

Children of the heavenly Father
Become baptized, sealed with a cross.

Whose sacrifice is this?

Women weep at the sight of Christ on the cross.
Offenses to God are remembered.

The words of institution are said.
Wine and bread are offered.
The blood of Christ shed for you.
The Body of Christ given for you.
Whose blood is shed? Whose body is given?

Sermons blast at the core of humanity
Framed in sexist slanted language.
The raped become convicted
The molested become ashamed.

The perpetrator escorts his family out
Relieved by his perfunctory participation.

Whose betrayal is this?

In the name of the Mother,
and of the Daughter,
and of the Holy Spirit.

Have mercy on us. Amen[5]

Frampton shows how survivors of family violence often perceive the symbols of patriarchy in worship and the Eucharist. The sin of violence goes unlabeled and unspoken in church. Women are silenced and ignored and asked to confess their sins and forgive their abusers. When the bread and wine become the body and blood of Christ, Frampton asks: "Whose blood is shed? Whose body is broken?" Survivors have suffered real injuries that involved blood and broken bones and spirits. The result of this theology is that those who are raped are convicted of guilt while the perpetrator is relieved by his perfunctory participation.

Some survivors have decided to leave the Christian church. Some have moved to the Unitarian Universalists, the Unity Church, or the Quakers because their spirituality is not focused on the cross even though Jesus continues to be an inspiring figure. Others practice Wicca and other pre-Christian practices that empower women in different ways. Some are attracted to Asian religions with their practices of meditation and wisdom.

Can you list some ways the cross can be used to support abuse?

FEMINIST THEOLOGICAL REFLECTIONS

What do we say to survivors when they question the teachings of their pastors on the cross? How do we support survivors of violence when they seek empowerment? How do we accompany them as they challenge traditional understandings of the cross and search for new meanings? Wonhee Anne Joh, a Korean American theologian, states the problem bluntly: "I would like to examine the complex ways in which a traditional understanding of the cross (1) has perpetuated subjection and submission to self-abnegation as a 'true' sign of Christian discipleship and (2) continues to be embraced as a sign of challenge to those very dynamics of subjection, submission, and powerlessness."[6] Some feminist theologians[7] suggest that we help survivors find texts that focus on subjects besides the cross and Jesus' suffering. For example, some significant feminist interpretations have been done on texts from the Hebrew Bible and the Christian New Testament. The story of Tamar in 2 Samuel 13 is a favorite because Tamar's voice is a clear statement of Hebrew resistance to sexual violence. It is also a tragic story because the rape of Tamar leads to silence and disappearance. Marie Fortune calls it a memorial story to women who have resisted sexual violence for centuries. Fortune also directs attention to the story of Queen Vashti in the first chapter of Esther. Vashti refuses to dance in front of the king and his male friends even though it costs her the throne. In a similar way, Susanna resists rape by two priests in Daniel 13 and is vindicated by Daniel's vision of her innocence. Fortune suggests that there is a long tradition of women's resistance that unmasks the violence within patriarchy and supports the resistance of women today to acts of violence against them.[8] One way we can help survivors is by showing them stories of biblical resistance to violence that they can use for their healing journey.

Rita Nakashima Brock and Rebecca Parker suggest that the crucifixion needs to be decentered from the theology and worship of the church. They suggest that the cross is best interpreted as a tragic event without redeeming value. As evidence for their perspective, they show that the cross was not always the center of worship and practice for the church. Before the eleventh century, instead of a cross on the altar, there was usually a scene of the resurrection or ascension. One can see vestiges of these traditions in some churches in Europe. I visited a church in Wroclaw, Poland, in which there was no cross in front of the church. Rather, there was a statue of Jesus ascending into paradise. The message to the people is that if we follow Jesus, we will also ascend into paradise and be with God. Brock and Parker suggest that these images of resurrection and paradise would help contextualize and relativize the stories of the crucifixion and remove some of the obstacles that encourage violence against women.[9] So, a way to help survivors in

their religious life is to help them focus on the resurrection story and the possibilities of resurrection for believers today.

Some womanist theologians— namely, Delores Williams, Jacquelyn Grant, Kelley Brown Douglas,

List some Scriptures that can empower women who are being abused.

and JoAnne Terrell—feel obligated to keep the cross in the center of faith and worship because of the witness of African American women over many centuries. They quote historical sources that show Jesus' suffering and death is an important point of identification for women under the oppression of slavery and racism. Jacquelyn Grant presents one witness from an unknown slave woman:

> Come to us, Master Jesus. The sun is too hot; the road is long and sandy, and we don't have a buggy to send and fetch you. But Master, you remember how you walked that hard walk up Calvary and you weren't weary but thought about us all that way. We know you are not too weary to come to us. We pick out the thorns, the prickles, the briars, the backsliding and the quarrels and the sin out of your path so they won't hurt your pierced feet any more.[10]

Here a woman in the midst of suffering the violence of slavery identifies with Jesus who suffered and understands her suffering. She finds comfort that God is with her in her suffering. Kelly Brown Douglas begins her quest for a womanist Christology by remembering her grandmother's confession of faith:

> Reflecting back on my grandmother's faith, I now realize that she must have trusted that the Christ she prayed to had a special appreciation of her condition. This was a Christ who seemingly identified with a poor Black woman in her day-to-day struggle just to make it. Mama was certain that this Christ cared about the trials and tribulations of an ordinary Black woman. Christ empowered her to get through each day with dignity.[11]

Delores Williams believes that the cross must be reinterpreted as a symbol of liberation. The whole context of Jesus' life and teachings is an example of "how to live peacefully, productively, and abundantly in relationship. . . . Humankind is therefore redeemed through Jesus' life and not through Jesus' death. . . . As Christians, black women cannot forget the cross. But neither can they glorify it. To do so is to make their exploitation sacred. To do so is to glorify sin."[12] JoAnne Terrell adds her slightly different interpretation about how the cross can be helpful to survivors:

> Anyone's death has saving significance inasmuch as we learn continuously from the life that preceded it. . . . Those countless black women who suffer abuse and die at the hands of patriarchal, violence-driven persons—whose deaths go unreported and underreported, unprosecuted and underprosecuted—are potentially liberating for women if we learn from their experiences, if we see how they exercised or did not exercise their moral and creative agency. This seems a much more relevant view of the atoning worth of women's blood.[13]

In these womanist theologies, we see an alternative interpretation of the cross that does not diminish its violent, sinful causes, but reinterprets it as a symbol of liberation. The witness of the faithful is that God in Jesus represents life and healing. And although Jesus was killed on the cross by the patriarchal empire of the time, God's commitment to life survived. Therefore, if we find ourselves victims of violence, God will be with us and will never give up on us. We can go on in faith because healing and new life is always possible through human solidarity and personal courage. The witness of survivors from the past is that God is faithful in the midst of violence.

Sharon Thornton, a white feminist pastoral theologian,[14] gives examples of oppressed people who feel God's solidarity with their suffering when they meditate on the cross. One example is Mercy Amba Oduyoye from Nigeria: "Women in Africa know that they will need to be ready to risk even death in order to resist death. . . . 'They face the cross in the hope that the humanity of women will rise from the silence and peace of the graveyard.'"[15] For those who are oppressed, the cross can be empowering since it provides assurance that God knows about

> How can the cross be reinterpreted as a symbol of personal liberation?

their suffering and does not abandon them in their isolation. "Seeing the relationship between one's own suffering and the social conditions that create and perpetuate it can help people find new descriptions and alternative meaning for themselves."[16]

Korean theologian Chung Hyun Kyung writes about a similar witness from Filipino women:

> Jesus is neither a masochist who enjoys suffering, nor a father's boy who blindly does what he is told to do. On the contrary, Jesus is a compassionate man of integrity who identified himself with the oppressed. He "stood for all he taught and did" and took responsibility for the consequences of his choices even at the price of his life. This image of Jesus' suffering gives Asian women the wisdom to differentiate between the suffering imposed by an oppressor and the suffering that is the consequences of one's stand for justice and human dignity.[17]

Thornton takes an additional step when she suggests that the cross can be a symbol of liberation for abusers who are responsible for the suffering of others:

> For those who hold power over others in a particular society, the political cross speaks the word of judgment and demands change, usually in the form of relinquishment of power and control, followed by acts of reparation for past wrongs. . . . It pronounces judgment in the hope for *metanoia* on the part of the abusers. Judgment speaks the word that only God is God, and no one else is God.[18]

Deanna Thompson believes that it is possible to develop a feminist theology of the cross based on a reconstruction of the theology of Martin Luther. She acknowledges the problems with Luther's Christology—his use of sexist language like "harlot" for humanity, his betrayal of the peasants who stood up for their human rights, and his view of sin as making humans completely unworthy to have a relationship with God. Thompson agrees that these images contribute to violence against women in contemporary times.

Thompson says that there are four ways in which Luther's theology of the cross can be retrieved for women today: (a) *The cross can be seen as a critical principle that challenges all human authorities, institutions, and ideologies.* Luther's theology of the cross was intended as a critique of the theology of glory of the dominant Roman Catholic Church of the sixteenth century, and it can serve this function today. (b) *The cross can be seen as a symbol of solidarity with women who are victims of violence.* In this way, the image of the Crucified Woman[19] is a contemporary equivalent of Luther's theology, an image that is predominant among African American and Latino Christian women. (c) *The cross can be understood as a mirror of the human condition,* similar to Wonhee Joh's use of the word *abjection.* Many human beings know the reality of being defeated by life and are unable to pull ourselves out of trouble by our own efforts. The cross can symbolize the religious experience of total abjection, and communicate God's understanding of human finitude and sin. (d) *The cross can be understood as a symbol of friendship* in the sense used in the Gospel of John: "No one has greater love than this, to lay down one's life for one's friends" (John 15:13). In Jesus on the cross, we see a depth of friendship that is necessary to overcome the differences between God and humans.[20]

Kathryn Tanner suggests that the cross is best understood within the context of the patristic and later debates about the Trinity. She suggests that some feminists misunderstand the meaning of the cross because they forget about two principles that must be true in the God-human relationship: first, that God and humans have a noncompetitive relationship; and second, that God is radically transcendent in a way that undercuts most human generalizations about God. The center of these principles is the absolute generosity of God that is impossible for humans to understand or practice. That is, God gives life and existence to humans without becoming diminished. God is transcendent in such a way that God can give in a fully generous way without lacking anything as God. God is not diminished when humans increase. In the same way, the three persons of the Trinity give and receive from one another without losing anything of themselves. This type of transcendence, generosity, and noncompetitiveness is hard for humans to comprehend since we seem to live in a world characterized by scarcity, and humans always fear not having enough. Because of our finitude as humans, we are dependent on God's generosity in a way that frightens us and tempts us to try to secure our own survival. Such temptation is the root of sin and human evil. In contrast, the generosity of God to humans is unlimited and noncompetitive. We glimpse the reality of God's gift of life when we are involved in genuinely loving relationships where mutuality means an increase in value and beauty for everyone without loss for anyone. While we see this reality only in glimpses, it is a revelation of the internal life of the Trinity and the essential meaning of human life in relationship with God.[21]

Within this understanding of God and humanity, the cross of Christ has a different meaning than usually understood. As a fully human being, Jesus' crucifixion was an act of solidarity with humans. Because of his commitments to the disciples, the poor, and transformation of the religious and political systems, Jesus became a victim of human sin and evil. He was killed because he loved people who were oppressed and threatened the power and authorities of the world who depended on terror and passivity. As Tanner writes, "Jesus' death is a consequence of the life he led on behalf of others in a sinful world."[22] Because Jesus is fully divine, however, "death (and the sin that brought it) cannot conquer [Jesus] because of the relation with God in Christ. . . . Jesus saves therefore *as* a human being—for example, in and through the fact that he goes to the cross and comes out alive."[23] In the cross we see the transcendent generosity of God and God's noncompetitiveness with human beings. As fully human and divine, Jesus can go to the cross and survive because Jesus is unified with the transcendent generosity of God. Human salvation is possible because we can be unified with Christ, and this unity can be lived out in generous and noncompetitive relationships with others. Tanner stresses, "The Persons of the Trinity give to one another without suffering loss; each continues to have what it gives to others. . . . We too should give to others out of our own fullness."[24] We have received our life from the generous God. When we live in unity with Christ, we can give our life for others without losing the gifts that God has given us. Rather than being depleted by our giving, the way of mutual giving and receiving we have in Christ means an increase in life and beauty for all.

> How can the resurrection provide hope for those in captivity to domestic violence?

SUMMARY

A central problem in Christian theology is human sin and evil. God has created the world for good; but human sin and evil have corrupted the creation so that it is too frequently characterized by violence. Survivors of violence complain about the use of theology to perpetuate their violence by advocating submission, premature forgiveness, obedience, and suffering like Jesus on the cross. Feminist theologians have responded to these complaints with sympathy and various constructive proposals. The question of Christology is what God has done in Jesus Christ that saves humans from evil and transforms humans to fulfill their creative purpose, and what human responses move toward communion with God's purposes. Given the review of other theologies, I share my own constructive proposal on Christology in the next chapter.

FOUR
Constructing a Process Christology

I believe in Jesus Christ, a divine and human being, who fully embod-
ies the reality of God and humanity and discloses for humans both
the character of God and the character of human life in the world. In
the Scriptures, we see Jesus as a human being with extraordinary love
and sensitivity for the full web of human and natural life. Because his
attachment to life was shown in his actions of healing, teaching, and
challenges to evil, Jesus was beloved by the people. Because of his truth
telling and nonviolent symbolic confrontations of those with dominat-
ing power, he was crucified. Because of the resilient love and power
of God, Jesus was resurrected and lives today to lure the faithful into
communion with God and to reveal the stature of human life that
is possible through communion with God. "Christ has died; Christ
has risen; Christ will come again"—these liturgical words call us to
embrace the historical reality and the real presence of Jesus Christ, the
second member of the Trinity. Through Christ humanity is healed
from the ravages of evil and transformed for ministries with others.
Jesus Christ revealed that God and humans are relational, ambiguous,
and resilient in the midst of evil.

In this chapter, I confess my own understanding of what God has done
in Jesus Christ that saves humans from evil and transforms humans to
fulfill their creative purpose, and what human responses move toward
communion with God's purposes and salvation for the world.

Jesus is unique for Christians because he reveals the character of
God and the character of human beings. The stories we have received
about his life reveal a person who in many different circumstances
showed loving sensitivity that moved toward communion with self, others, and God and who engaged in loving creativity that moved toward
enlarged freedom for self, others, and God.[1]

Jesus had what theologian Bernard Meland calls "an attachment to life."[2] Within process theology, this means that Jesus was able to give his full attention to the flow of the human experiences of others in all their complexity, and to respond creatively in ways that revealed a quality of truth and value that set people free. Bernard Loomer says that Jesus engaged in relationships that were able to overcome the contradictions of love and hate, life and death, in ways that seemed impossible before he came.[3] Kathryn Tanner says that Jesus revealed that God is generous and merciful toward humanity, and that humans are capable of more generosity and mercy than they typically think is possible.[4] In this sense, Jesus revealed the size of God and the size of humanity and the nature of the divine-human relationship.[5] Jesus was important, according to Christian tradition, because his revelation about God and humans was a qualitatively new concept of God in human history, an emergent truth that had never been disclosed before. Jesus' life, death, and resurrection brought God and humanity together in a new, reconciled way, and revealed new possibilities for human faith and action.[6] What is the image of God and humanity we see in Jesus Christ?

> Where do you see Jesus' "attachment to life" in the stories from the New Testament?

JESUS AS RELATIONAL

According to Scripture, Jesus said seven "words" on the cross before he died: "I am thirsty" (John 19:28); "Forgive them; for they do not know what they are doing" (Luke 22:34); "Woman, here is your son" (John 19:26); "My God, My God, why have you forsaken me?" (Matt. 27:46; Mark 15:34); "It is finished" (John 19:30); "You will be with me in paradise" (Luke 23:43); "Father, into your hands I commend my spirit" (Luke 23:46).

I submit that these sentences reveal Jesus' attachment to life—his loving sensitivity and loving creativity.[7] In the midst of violence and personal crisis, Jesus showed that he was deeply engaged in his relationships. He was aware of his body and its crisis of life and death; he was aware of the soldiers who were committing atrocities, and of two human

beings next to him who were perpetrators and victims of violence; he
was aware of his mother at the foot of the cross, and of his relationship
with God; he was aware of the moment of his death, and of his future
with God. At the moment of greatest crisis in his life, Jesus was fully
sensitive to the relationships within which he was embedded in all their
tragic meaning and value.

Traditional theology has too often been built on the premise that
there is something wrong with relationships because they are finite and
constantly changing. Many Christian believers seek what is eternal.
This has often meant the hatred of the body and the development of a
hierarchy of human power to distinguish between those whose lives are
subject to finitude and those who are able to transcend their circumstances through education, fine arts, and wealth. Much human evil can
be traced to this binary distinction of eternity and finitude, and its cor-
ollary dualities of mind and body, matter and spirit, male and female,
white and nonwhite.

In contrast, Jesus embraced the temporal relationships of his life.
Scripture shows that he was fully engaged in the moment and with the
persons who surrounded him at the time. He was challenged and put to
the test by the conflicting forces he encountered. He responded in parables and unexpected words that reframed the assumptions and expectations of others. To the question about paying taxes, he said, "Render
to Caesar the things that are Caesar's, and to God the things that are
God's" (Mark 12:17, KJV). When confronted about healing on the
Sabbath, he responded, "The sabbath was made for humankind, and
not humankind for the sabbath" (Mark 2:27). Expected to defer to the
Sadducees and Pharisees because of their status in the Jewish society, he
challenged them with the contradictions of their own arguments (Matthew 23). The stories of Jesus have remained compelling for many centuries because of his total engagement in the relational moment. Jesus
showed the power of God and the Spirit as fully and radically relational.

Jesus also was fully in touch with the larger social systems around
him—the culture, religion, politics, and economics of his life situation.
His commitment to symbolic nonviolent resistance was acutely in tune
with the hopes and fears of an oppressed people within the context of
a brutal Roman Empire and a corrupt indigenous elite. The injustice
of the colonial system was a focus of many of his teachings and miracles. He advocated forgiveness of the people for the debts they had

incurred through unjust taxes and loss of their lands. He forgave the
people their sin defined by the religious system whose economy was
based on receiving sacrifices at the Temple. He fed the hungry to reveal
the generosity of God toward those who were not considered human
enough to share the wealth of the land. He healed the sick without
going through the doctors and priests and paying for approved religious
rituals. He preached that tax collectors and prostituted women would
enter the kingdom of God ahead of the ordained religious leaders who
were corrupt. He delivered prophetic judgments against the Sadducees
who had stolen resources for themselves and taken the land of the poor.
He threatened to tear down the Temple and rebuild it in three days. He
taught his disciples an alternative way of perceiving and interacting with
the world. In all of these words and actions, he showed a keen awareness of the way power was constructed at the social level, and clearly put
himself with the company of the great prophets who condemned Israel
for its corruption in the past. In these ways, Jesus showed himself to be
fully human and fully engaged in relationships with people and society.

Jesus revealed the depth of "relational power," the ability to engage
in mutual relationships that enhanced communion with self, others,
and God. He was fully creative in responding to what he was given.
He perceived the contradictions in the lives of persons and systems and
responded in ways that enlarged freedom for those who took him seriously. For those who had ears to hear, he spoke directly and authorita-
tively: the whole law is fulfilled in this commandment, to love God and
to love your neighbor as yourself (Matt. 22:39). For those who were
blinded by their own interests and sin, he spoke in parables: "Which
of these . . . was a neighbor to the one who fell into the hands of the
robbers? . . . Go and do likewise" (Luke 10:36-37). Jesus received the
impact of others on his deepest being and then responded with creativity so that they could be larger and freer than before.

Because of these characteristics, the stories of Jesus remain compelling today as examples of what it means to be fully human. We can be
fully human and in communion with God when we also have an attachment to life by receiving the complex relationships of those around us
and responding in creative ways that lead to communion and enlarged
freedom for all.

In addition to revealing the nature of full humanity, Jesus reveals
God to be fully and radically relational as well. According to process

thought, God is a vital part of every moment of becoming, offering to each moment potentially creative possibilities, and receiving into Godself the final synthesis of individual decisions. We have communion with God when we are attached to our relationships in the way that God is attached. In these moments we are in communion

> How can we be fully human and in communion with God within our complex relationships with others and respond in creative ways that lead to communion and enlarged freedom for all?

with self, others, and God. In his life and death, Jesus discloses full humanity and full divinity for those who have eyes to see. Such a perspective informs some of the most interesting theologies of the Trinity.

Survivors of violence know the impact of relationships on their lives—the good, the bad, and the ugly. Because they experienced abuse of power that damaged their bodies and spirits, they know the impact of trauma on the formation of their lives. Most survivors I have talked with also experienced loving power through relationships that provided resources they needed for healing. They know that both good and evil come from relationships. And while most survivors I know well went through a period in their lives when they rejected relationships because they were too painful, they returned to the relational web because they wanted to become full human beings again.

JESUS AS AMBIGUOUS

Jesus was and is an ambiguous figure and reveals that God's love and power are ambiguous. To the extent that Jesus was fully human, he participates in the ambiguity of all human life. If we can understand the ambiguity of human life, we may better understand the ambiguity of Jesus.[9]

According to Loomer, life has inherent ambiguity. By ambiguity, he means there are divisions within life itself. There does not seem to be a single purpose toward the good in the concreteness of life. Rather, "the world of our experience is at odds with itself."[10] This arises out of his observation "that our world, especially at the human level, is filled with evil and ambiguous elements which thwart and bedevil the noblest purposes of God and [humans]."[11] There are three ways in which human life is ambiguous.

First, *ambiguity arises through the multiplicity of influences in the lives of individuals and societies.* Individual human experiences emerge within a relational context as a confluence of competing and conflicting influences. Our moments of experience do not develop in a void, but in the midst of decisions we have made in the past and the direct influence of decisions of other people. Each moment becomes what it is in the middle of a muddle. Over time, the decisions we make include many unresolved conflicts and even contradictions. We try to make the best decisions we can, but every decision is fraught with tension, and in crisis situations we are faced with contradictions that cannot be resolved. Often we passively accept the tensions since there seems no way to resolve them. Individuals and societies emerge from the claims of many relationships. In the integration of these relationships, a single decision is the result, but "it need not be singleminded."[12] Within the decision there will be ambivalence, that is, the presence of two or more conflicting feelings at once. There is no escape from these claims because of the essential social nature of experience, and this reality leads to ambiguity in human life. It is difficult for an individual or society to be unambiguously for the good because of the deep ambivalence inherited from the past into each occasion of experience.

Second, *ambiguity arises through the tension between the relationality and freedom within human existence.* The individual emerges from its relationships with a drive toward creative freedom. In some ways, freedom is encouraged by the relationality of existence because it is part of the restlessness toward greater size. But freedom has an untamed and wild side that threatens to expand beyond its relationships and create instability. At the same time the relationality of life puts limits on freedom and threatens its existence by demanding that it be definite and concrete. So there are contrasting drives, one toward expansion, the other toward containment. "On the one hand there is a restlessness to continue the advance to a more complex stage even though this effort requires a finer and more demanding discipline. On the other side there is an impulse to rest and be content with the good which has been achieved."[13]

The impulse of freedom pulls toward more diversity with the threat of instability, while the impulse of relationality pushes toward stability with the threat of stagnation. Every advance endangers the stability, and every satisfaction endangers the advance. The result, according to Loomer, is that "in many instances the higher levels of achievement become increasingly fragile in their constitution."[14] Greater size demands an openness to new possibilities that make human life vulnerable to contradictions which would destroy persons and communities. Thus, freedom and relationality have an inherent conflict that creates ambiguity in life.

Third, *ambiguity as the mixture of good and evil is "found at the core of the human spirit."*[15] Human life has simultaneous drives toward realizing new potentials and living the full life, but also fearing the success of greater size and withdrawing from life in self-defense. From another perspective, the good and the evil in a person are actually the same thing. The strengths of a person that can lead to greater size are also weaknesses that can create a dangerous pride and selfishness. The tendency to excel in one endeavor can become a rigidity that leads to destruction of other possibilities. Depth psychology has clearly shown that the life force of a person often correlates with the shadow side of personality, and one must be able to face both the good and evil in oneself in order to make use of one's potential. This ambiguity cannot be eliminated without also destroying the very impulses of life.

With this analysis, Loomer has identified ambiguity in the concreteness of human life. In its existential form, life is ambivalent, at odds with itself, and a mixture of good and evil to its core. Much human trouble can be traced to this

What are the three kinds of ambiguity in human life? Where do you see these ambiguities in your own life?

ambiguity and the confusion it creates as individuals and societies make decisions that try to move toward "qualitative richness."[16]

Two examples of this ambiguity in narratives about Jesus are nonviolence and the cross. When Jesus began preaching to the crowds and calling the disciples, he called for repentance. While we often interpret these doctrines in the United States in spiritual and interpersonal ways, I think Jesus meant them also as political doctrines. By repentance, Jesus meant that the people should withdraw their allegiance from the religious and political authorities of the day and redefine their identities as moral and political agents in relationships with God, self, and others.

John was baptizing for repentance, and when Jesus submitted to John's baptism, he was taking a public vow that he would give his allegiance only to God. [17] This is the meaning of his statement, "Render to Caesar the things that are Caesar's, and to God the things that are God's" (Mark 12:17, KJV). When leaders do the will of God, one can give loyalty to both God and leaders. But the human and divine empires are often in conflict with one another and humans are faced with choices that shape personal identity. Many from the crowds that heard Jesus and the disciples who followed him were attracted by his critique of the religious and political authorities. Jesus' words and actions were a constant critique of the oppression and corruption that caused the suffering of the people.

In a similar way, Jesus offered liberation for the people in the context of the religious and political oppression of the time. The people were kept enslaved by taxes from Rome, by their financial debts to the Temple, and by their uncleanness as defined by religious laws. There was no way poor people could remain righteous given the purity codes from the Temple, and restoring righteousness required expensive sacrifices and gifts to the priests. Therefore, advocating forgiveness of debts and sins was a direct attack on the systems that kept the people enslaved. Because of Jesus' liberation theology, the crowds and disciples followed him.

However, the crowds and the disciples could not understand Jesus and eventually rejected his road to the cross and his commitment to nonviolence. When the crowds saw that Jesus was not planning a military attack on the Temple, and when they realized that Jesus did not use his power to violently change the systems he had preached against, they felt betrayed and abandoned his movement. They did not understand that Jesus had another vision of how humans can live together that was not based in terror and violence. In a similar way, the disciples were slow to understand Jesus' methods. When they argued about who would have the favored seats in Jesus' new government, Jesus rebuked them and tried to teach them about servanthood. They rejected his teachings about the probability of suffering and death for those who would point to a different way. They were moved by the foot-washing and bread-and-cup ceremony in the upper room, but did not understand what they symbolized (John 13). They slept through the prayers in Gethsemane because they had no idea that Jesus' active ministry was nearly over.

Before the crucifixion and resurrection the crowds and the disciples did not accept Jesus' teaching about nonviolence. Yet as my ancestors, the Anabaptists and Pietists, read the Scriptures, they saw Jesus' teachings about nonviolence throughout the Gospels: blessed are the peacemakers; blessed are the meek; blessed are those who are persecuted for righteousness; do not be angry with your neighbor; do not return evil for evil; those who live by the sword will die by the sword; you ought to wash one another's feet; forgive them for they do not know what they are doing; which one was a neighbor to the one in need? My religious ancestors were convinced

Why is the nonviolence of Jesus is a hard teaching for humans to accept?

that Jesus taught and practiced nonviolence, and that nonviolence was a central mark of the church. I have learned this truth since my childhood; indeed, Christian pacifism goes back through seven generations in my family. My people have believed and tried to practice nonviolence based on the imitation of Jesus' nonviolent teachings.

Nonviolence is a hard teaching for humans to accept. Many militant forms of Christianity today teach that God is a judge who will destroy those who are evil, and that Christians are authorized by God to attack and destroy evil and evil people in God's name.[18] The majority of the world's Christian community rejects nonviolence because human beings cannot imagine the world without the use of violent power. Since empires maintain their power through terror and violence, this must be the only way to survive and gain liberation. Jesus' doctrine of nonviolence is one example of God's ambiguity. From a human point of view, violence seems an inevitable and God-given method of controlling evil and evil people in this world. Therefore, Jesus' commitment to nonviolence seems full of ambiguity and impracticalities at a human level.

How can the cross be understood as an example of Jesus' ambiguity?

Another example of Jesus' ambiguity is the crucifixion symbolized in the cross. For the crowds and the disciples, the crucifixion was a tragic failure and an end to their hopes and dreams for the coming of the kingdom of God. What sense could the disciples make of the crucifixion? It

was not until the moment of Pentecost that an interpretation of the crucifixion as an important symbol of God's faithfulness began to emerge,
and through the power of the Holy Spirit the disciples lost their fear and
began speaking out in public. Peter said: "This man . . . you crucified
and killed by the hands of those outside the law. But God raised him
up"[19] (Acts 2:23-24). Since that moment, various interpretations of the
crucifixion have emerged, and today the discussion on the meaning of
the cross is as contested and lively as ever, as we saw in the previous chapter. Unfortunately, some doctrines of the cross have been turned into
symbols of oppression and violence against the most vulnerable persons
in our world—the poor, women, and others who lack the religious and
political power to define and defend themselves.

What are we to make of Jesus' teaching about nonviolence and the
event of the crucifixion? These are crucial questions for faith and they
illustrate the ambiguity of God's morality from a human point of view.

I believe that ambiguity goes deep into the character of the Trinity
and does not stop with human understanding. The doctrine of emergence in process theology is used by Bernard Meland to counteract the
view that all novelty is already contained in the mind of God just wait-
ing for the opportunity to become realized in concrete reality. In contrast, Meland believed that God and humans together create novelty,
and that even the mind of God cannot anticipate and control what
happens in this divine-human interaction:

> Emergence in its profound meaning is never simply change; it is re-creation
> or re-conception. It is a transformative occurrence in which the elements of
> an older structure are thrust into a new order of relations. . . . Yet the good is
> always in the act of qualitative attainment wherein emergence wrests from past
> structures the qualifying influence which can be assimilated into the new.[20]

God's moral ambiguity is based in the fact that there is no goodness,
even in God, that can exhaust the novelty that is possible in the world,
and that every profound novelty is an expansion of previous definitions
of goodness. Ambiguity, by definition, is a mixture of good and evil in
a way that is confusing and painful for the subject. Yet, according to my
view, ambiguity is the very way that novel morality occurs within the
processes of time and history.[21]

I submit that nonviolence and the crucifixion are examples of God's
ambiguity. The fact that these symbols continue to be contested and

fought over shows their ambiguous reality. God interacts with humans in a way that humans perceive as ambiguous, and God's interaction is in fact ambiguous because it strives for a novel goodness that has so far been impossible in history.

Nonviolence and ambiguity are novel ideas that were emphasized in Jesus' ministry and reemphasized in the reality of crucifixion and resurrection. Jesus' decision not to fight against the corrupt authorities, and his refusal to incite the crowds and his disciples to military resistance, or to bring down thousands of angels to defend him, are ambiguous to those who believe that military action is the only way to control evil. They continue to be controversial and ambiguous actions today.

Charismatic Christian groups have arisen throughout history to reaffirm Jesus' principles of nonviolence—monastic groups of the Middle Ages, Franciscans, Hutterites and Moravians, Mennonites and Quakers from the Reformation, Brethren from the Pietistic reforms, and many utopian communities since the Enlightenment and Romantic periods of Western history. But nonviolence is hardly unique to Christianity. Nonviolence is reaffirmed by various groups within Buddhism, Hinduism, and many other religious traditions. In a sense Jesus, during his life, joined a great host of mystics and saints who taught and practiced nonviolence as the way of God. The Mennonites believe that there has been an unbroken succession of martyrs in every generation since Jesus whose witness has preserved nonviolence as a theory and practice.[22] Nonviolence has been practiced and reaffirmed in my lifetime by Gandhi, Martin Luther King Jr., and by nonviolent revolutions in South Africa, the Philippines, and other countries. Yet, nonviolence remains an ambiguous symbol and strategy. Why? Because most human beings do not believe that evil in the world can be defeated except by violence, and because human beings believe they have the right to power and control over others.

Domestic violence is a test of ideas about nonviolence and the cross. Upon hearing that a child has been physically or sexually abused, most humans feel a compelling urge to defend the one who is vulnerable and punish the abuser. Those who cannot protect themselves from harm should be defended and abusers should be held accountable for their abuse of power—ethical principles accepted by most human beings. However, self-defense and defense of the vulnerable is frequently used as a justification for violence. Most humans believe that the world is dangerous and we must be prepared to use violence because it is the only way to protect ourselves or someone who is vulnerable from harm.

Survivors of violence are keenly aware that there are deep ambiguities in a commitment to violence as a form of self-defense. First, when we experience violence from another, intense contradictions between our will to live conflict with the desire of another to spread terror. How can we make the choice for life in the face of terror? Violence promotes fear and rage that can easily work against creative love in our lives. We are faced with the choice of whether to imitate those who force their violence on us. The relational matrix for survivors of domestic violence shows the deep contradictions between a wish for peace and integrity versus a wish for revenge and power over another. As survivors move through the stages of healing, they encounter moments when the conflict between a desire for peace and the wish to do violence seem unbearable. Paradoxically, it is the moment of greatest tension that creates the possibility of a novel way of understanding one's relationships and personal identity. What kind of person do I want to be, and how will I bring together the contradictions I have inherited from the past?

> Is self-defense a sufficient justification for the use of violence?

A second ambiguity lies in the social implications of our decisions of whether to defend ourselves or those who are vulnerable by using violence. What kind of consequences do we create by choosing either passivity or violence within a particular moment? René Girard says that the primary cause of social violence in the world is imitation of the violence of others. We organize our desires according to those persons we admire, and we adopt their methods for fulfilling these desires. When we see someone we admire using violence, we rationalize our own use of violence. We see the advantages of using violence to get what we want, so we imitate one who has used violence to get things we want for ourselves. In this way, violence becomes an organized social pattern. Mimetic violence quickly becomes a mechanism for oppressing those who are vulnerable to make ourselves feel more powerful and more bonded with those we love.

Girard says that violence can be prevented when the mimesis underlying violence is disrupted by those who are mature enough to absorb violence without becoming violent themselves. For Girard and other scholars, Jesus' decision to face death on the cross rather than call down thousands of angels to defend him is the primary example of how the mechanism underlying violence can be destroyed. The cross becomes, for Girard, the introduction of novelty into history. Jesus self-consciously decides not to defend himself with violence even though he is innocent. Thus, he shows that nonviolence is humanly possible, and he reveals the bankruptcy of the idea that violence is justified by self-defense, a form of mimesis.[23]

A third ambiguity in our decision on whether to use violence is that the same impulses that energize our wish to live and protect others can become impulses to destroy another through violence. That is, we decide in particular moments of stress who we are in that moment. Our decisions create our personal identity. We cannot split ourselves up so that the part that chooses violence is detached from the part of us that chooses life. Every decision we make forms our personal identity. When we decide to use violence, we are incorporating violence into our identity in ways that cannot be separated out from the rest of ourselves. Violence introduces a contradiction into our lives that requires resolution, and no amount of rationalization will take away the stain that violence creates.[24] Facing the deep ambiguities in ourselves between violence and nonviolence determines our character and decides whether we will have novelty to offer to the future, or just more of the same long history of violence.

Jesus was faced with many temptations to use violence: when Satan offered him worldly power in exchange for worship; when he saw the hunger and illness of the poor that was unaddressed by those with money; when he heard the hypocrisy of the religious leaders who took money from the poor without helping them; when he faced the betrayals and plots to take his life and destroy the hopes of the people; when he was accused, tortured, and tried for crimes he did not commit. Yet in each moment, Jesus received the violence from others, considered the social implications of his decisions, and chose his identity as a non-violent child of God. Jesus went to the cross in order to disrupt the violence of his time organized into personal attitudes, social institutions, and religious practices. And his message of nonviolence survives today whenever believers rediscover the core message of his life and death. In his resurrection his decisions were confirmed by the love and power of God. No violence of human beings can destroy the resilience of God's love and power for the creation.

The suffering servant is rather one who has sustained a relationship involving great contrast, in this case the incompatibility between love and hate. In absorbing the hate or indifference derived from the other, while attempting to sustain the relationship by responding with love for the other, the extreme of contrasts is exemplified. This contrast is an incompatibility, in fact an emotional contradiction. But by having the size to absorb this contradiction within the integrity of his own being, and in having the strength to sustain the relationship, the incompatibility has been transformed into a compatible contrast.[25]

Survivors of violence report that one of their core struggles is whether they must identify with the violence of their abusers in order to appropriate enough power to live. In psychological theory, this is called "identification with the aggressor." Children who have been abused often identify with the most important person in their lives. Sadly, this is often the abuser. In fact, some survivors have chosen violence in response to experiences of abuse. I worked with one man who killed his abuser five years after the man had kidnapped and raped him over three days. Given the horrendous abuse he suffered, one could understand the murder as a form of self-defense. He served eight years in prison for that murder. I was seeing him because he had also abused several young boys in the community after he was released from prison. Taking revenge against his abuser had not resolved the issues of his own abuse. He killed an abuser, but then he became an abuser, imitating the very identity he hated.

Many survivors have worked through their temptations to violence and have chosen nonviolence as a way of developing an identity that differentiates them from the one who abused them. One of the most difficult parts of the healing is working through the many layers of internal violence until one can love again. Linda struggled for years with the idea that her mother was a part of her interior life and she would never be able to get rid of her influence, even though she had committed suicide many years earlier. Gradually, over time, her mother's power diminished as Linda chose nonviolence in her own life.

Sometimes survivors are pressured to forgive their abusers in ways that are dangerous for their safety and health. Linda never forgave her mother for what she did and the decades of damage she caused. For other survivors, the concept of forgiveness of the abuser has been helpful. Karen, another survivor I knew well, forgave her father for incest. However, her capacity for forgiveness happened after her father had become a very small influence in her life even though he was still living.[26] For all survivors the idea of forgiveness is ambiguous: some say they have forgiven and others reject the idea of forgiveness. For

What are the arguments for and against nonviolence as a central doctrine of Christology?

me, the crucial issue is not forgiveness, but the ability of the survivor to choose life and reject the violence that victimized them at such a vulnerable age.[27]

JESUS AS RESILIENT

Jesus reveals that God's love and power is resilient.[28] One of the main things I have learned from my ministry with survivors of sexual and domestic violence is the resilience of God and humans. This is the best concept I have found to understand the will to live and heal with survivors whose lives have been traumatized and damaged by abuse.

Linda Crockett writes about the "war zone" of her family home, which seemed similar to the war zone of El Salvador that she also experienced firsthand. During her several trips to El Salvador, she was present in villages when there was bombing from airplanes and when paramilitary troops terrorized the population.[29] She identified with the terror, captivity, and disconnection[30] of people during the war against the campesinos in El Salvador. From infancy until age twelve, she had experienced terror, captivity, and disconnection because of the sadistic and ritualized sexual abuse by her mother. Traveling to El Salvador twenty years after her childhood abuse had stopped, Linda recognized the signs of trauma. But it was the El Salvadoran faith and determination to survive that ignited the hope in her spirit. After days of listening to their understandings of what was happening and how they stuck together whether they lived or died, Linda dared to believe that there was a God of love and power who had not completely abandoned her. Based on their witness to hope, she entered into a journey of healing that was remarkable for me to witness.

Given the horror of the abuse she experienced and its lifetime effects, Linda should not be alive and thriving. She gives witness that it is only a miracle that she did not die at the hands of her mother, from the drugs she took in adolescence, or by the violence of one of the many men who systematically abused her during her teenage years. Even harder to comprehend is why her hope did not die. While the survival of her spirit cannot be explained, Linda survived and found healing. Now she is working as a trainer and speaker to provide resources so other survivors can make it.

I have seen the same resilient spirit when I talked with survivors of the Holocaust, survivors of torture from Latin America, survivors of poverty in Nicaragua, survivors of civil war in Africa and Korea. I have also seen this resilient spirit in some perpetrators I have worked with. In spite of the trauma of their childhoods and the sexual trauma they imposed on a child, they planned to be survivors and face up to the abuse from others and the internal evil they had acted on at another's expense. I have seen people do amazing things in situations where the human spirit should have been crushed. This does not mean that the spirits of some with similar experiences were not crushed. There are thousands of suicides and murders, and addicted, prostituted, homeless women and men every year because of child sexual abuse. These are the ones who did not survive to give witness to their stories. The ones who have survived and found healing give witness to the effects of violence and evil that claimed their sisters and brothers. That anyone survived some of the experiences of violence is miraculous. My own witness is that the human spirit is resilient far beyond our ability to understand it. And it is this spirit that forms the foundation of loving community.

I believe that the resilience of the human spirit reveals the resilience of the Spirit of God. Given the massive evil of the contemporary world, humans can reasonably ask whether God has abandoned the world. It is obvious that God does not prevent all human evil and its consequences. The total scope of violence against children and women is evidence that God does not always protect the most vulnerable persons against violence from their own families and their own governments. Apparently God does not override human freedom to protect the vulnerable. The question that is left is whether God in Godself survives the violence and provides hope for new life after violence.

Linda Crockett, the Lutherans of El Salvador, Holocaust survivors, and many others give witness that God's love and power is resilient. The life, death, and resurrection of Jesus give a similar message. Jesus taught and healed in order to communicate a new vision of God's love and power, and he worked to form a nonviolent community that would be faithful

Constructing a Process Christology

73

to this vision in the midst of violent, imperial evil. Jesus engaged in symbolic actions that challenged the legitimacy of the Roman Empire and their indigenous collaborators, including the Temple and its laws. When his actions and his popularity with the people were perceived as a real danger to those who benefited from the status quo, he was arrested, tried, tortured, and killed by the religious and political leadership. Through all

In what ways is Jesus' story a story of resilience?

of these stories, Jesus remained consistent in his vision of nonviolent community and refused to take up military action to further his goals and save his life. He died and was buried because of the evil actions of the leaders of his community. On the third day he rose from the dead and appeared to the disciples, reminding them of the vision he had taught them and exhorting them to carry on the work he had started. He sent them back to Galilee to preach and organize the people. In the event of Pentecost, the Holy Spirit entered into the people, took away their fear, and gave them words of power to speak to the people. In that moment the new religious movement commenced that has shaped my life today.

The cross reveals the abjection of evil[31] and its profound consequences—God was crucified.[32] The resurrection reveals the resilience of God's love and power. What appeared to the crowds, the disciples, and the enemies of Jesus as a defeat was not a total defeat. God did not protect Jesus from violence but allowed evil human beings and systems to kill him; God's Spirit in Jesus survived and came into full power at Pentecost. The spirit of Jesus that died survived and lived on in the people. Jesus went to the cross and came out alive.[33] I have seen this miracle in the lives of Linda Crockett, Philip, and my friends from Nicaragua, Sierra Leone, Korea, and Germany. In each case, the survivor was dead and yet she lived. God seemed to abandon them, yet God was with them to restore hope and provide resources for new life. Theologically, we might say that God in Jesus was crucified and resurrected to live on in heaven and in the faithful community that embodied his spirit. In a similar way God was abused with Linda and God's resilient love and power was with her when she regained hope of healing. Philip gave up many times, unable to face the internalized shame and externalized stigma of being a sex offender. His friendship is a gift to me that reminds me every time we talk that God's love and power are resilient.

Human freedom is real, and it creates the possibility of great human evil. God does not always intervene to prevent evil from enacting its cycle of destruction. But God's Spirit is resilient and available for human survivors and perpetrators when they are ready for new life. In this sense, God's Spirit can be killed, but it cannot be destroyed. And those human beings whose spirits have been crushed by violence yet survived can find solace and healing from God. As followers of Jesus, Christians are called to believe and embody the resilient Spirit of God in our ministries with those who are vulnerable. In our nonviolent resistance to evil, we may die, but we will live again in the courageous believers who follow us. In communion with God, we can receive God's generous love and power and share it with those whose resilient spirit has enabled them to survive horrendous things. Together in solidarity, believers can survive violence and transform the human spirit.

What does the resurrection symbolize for you? How do you see resilience at work in human life and faith?

SUMMARY

Jesus reveals God as relational, ambiguous, and resilient through his life, teachings, ministry, death, and resurrection. Jesus was radically relational in his attentiveness to immediate occasions of experience and his creative responses to the challenges he faced in his everyday life. Jesus showed receptive power in his ability to relate to the individuals who encountered him—the poor, religious leaders, and people at every level of society. He understood not only their subjective interior life but also the religio-political circumstances that made them who they were. Jesus lived with sensitivity that moved toward communion with self, others, and God, and with creativity that moved toward enlarged freedom for self, others, and God. His encounters were frequently transformative for others, and because of his intense power and love, his enemies feared him and sought to end his life. He was killed by the religious and political leaders and he survived through the resurrection. He appeared to the disciples and sent his partner, the Holy Spirit, to empower his disciples to continue his mission of nonviolent transformation of human consciousness and justice for all.

Jesus was morally ambiguous because his behaviors were based on
a transcendent morality that was beyond human understanding. His
teachings and miraculous signs were often astounding and confusing for
those around him. Jesus was also morally ambiguous because he sought a
kind of novelty that went beyond what had existed up to that time. Jesus
sought a nonviolent kingdom that revealed God's love and power, and
his movement was about a new morality as an emergent reality within
history. Jesus' teachings and symbolic actions of transcendence and nonviolence were then, and are today, ambiguous symbols for human life.
The majority of people in the world reject nonviolence as a viable political strategy, even though nearly everyone personally wishes for a local
community characterized by nonviolence. Every generation produces
new communities that embody the nonviolence of Jesus. Nonviolence
as an identity and strategy can be defeated, but it always returns. Jesus'
ambiguous teachings and actions have the potential for transformation
of the human spirit today.

Jesus reveals that God's love and power are resilient. Jesus lived and
died for his vision of a novel future, but Jesus could not be destroyed.
He died through crucifixion and was resurrected in heaven and on
earth. In heaven Jesus is a member of the Trinity that embodies the
generous nonviolent spirit that he spoke about. On earth Jesus lives on
through and beyond the community of those who believe in him and
follow him, the Christian church. Although the church is an ambiguous symbol of Jesus Christ, the vision that Jesus proposes is resurrected
from time to time within the church. New generations rediscover the
vision of Jesus because of the stories that are remembered and the rituals that are performed: worship, baptism, Eucharist, care, and mission.
Human evil and its systemic embodiments continue to promote violence and oppression of humans and the natural earth. But new forms
of the church regularly recover the original vision and make it available
for human transformation.

The next chapter explores the idea of the church empowered by the
Holy Spirit. What are the marks of the church when it is faithful to the
trinitarian God revealed in Jesus Christ?

FIVE
Faithful Churches
Empowered by the Holy Spirit

I believe in the Holy Spirit, the third person of the Trinity, who provides everyday empowerment for the world. The Spirit strengthens the resilience of human beings in the midst of the complex relationships and the moral ambiguity of daily life. The Holy Spirit redeems human and natural life. I believe the church is called to be the body of Christ, a community of bodies and spirits, of humans and nature, in communion with the Holy Spirit, with the following marks: (1) inclusive love, (2) empowering justice, (3) nonviolent resistance to evil, (4) multiplicity and unity, (5) ambiguity and goodness. Through worship, the sacraments of baptism and communion, and programs of care and prophetic witness, the true church creates a resilient witness of hope for a suffering world.

This chapter explores the question, What are the marks of the churches when they are faithful to God through Christ and empowered by the Holy Spirit? I use the plural, "faithful churches," to be consistent with the emphasis in this project on the complex relationality of human life and the moral ambiguity of living in a concrete world of material reality.

> What are the marks of the churches when they are faithful to God in Christ and empowered by the Holy Spirit?

There are many ways that churches claim faithfulness to the vision and memory of Jesus Christ, and sometimes they do not recognize one another as members of the same family. The history of the churches is filled with ambiguity:

1. the ambiguity of the Roman Catholic Church's compromises with empire and its crusades against Jews and Muslims;

2. the ambiguity of the Orthodox churches' accommodation to despotic regimes in the East;

3. the ambiguity of the Protestants in Europe and the United States, their support of the slave trade and slavery, their colonial missionary movements, and their support of U.S. military adventurism;

4. the ambiguity of the Pentecostal churches who often preach prosperity and election to the poorest people while taking their money.

All of these ambiguities are well documented and disturbing.

In this chapter I develop a normative set of marks based on Scripture, tradition, and religious experience that can guide our reflections on the nature of the diverse churches. Other writers develop criteria for the faithful churches that emphasize much different parts of the theological tradition. I lay out my own normative principles in hopes that I can be in conversations with those who come from other perspectives. The only truly authoritative statements about norms that would be inclusive of all churches would come from conversations that include all of the various communions. Such conversations are going on in the World Council of Churches, other international forums, and within national and regional groups. I consider my project as a contribution to these larger conversations.

THE HOLY SPIRIT

I use the term "empowered by the Holy Spirit" as a continuation of the previous discussion of the trinitarian God.[1] Theologically, the Holy Spirit is the least developed doctrine of the Trinity. The Holy Spirit is commonly associated with empowerment and often focused on the work of the churches. While the Holy Spirit works in hidden ways outside of the churches because of God's transcendence, the church is the community that claims the power of the Holy Spirit.

If a doctrine of the Holy Spirit has been forgotten among theologians in recent decades, it has never been forgotten among the people. Spiritual revivals have exploded all over the world as people seek religious answers to the alienation and oppression of their lives. From New

Age fascination with indigenous American, Asian, and African religions
to the enthusiastic and emotional Pentecostal theologies, people seek
knowledge of God through the Holy Spirit.

> The Holy Spirit is not simply the subjective side of God's revelation of [God]
> self, and faith is not merely the echo of the Word of God in the human heart.
> The Holy Spirit is much more than that. It is the power that raises the dead,
> the power of the new creation of all things; and faith is the beginning of the
> rebirth of human beings to new life. But this means that the Holy Spirit is by
> no means merely a matter of revelation. It has to do with life and its source.
> The Holy Spirit is called "holy" because it sanctifies life and renews the face
> of the earth.[2]

Bernard Meland defines "spirit" as the goodness of relationships in
human life: "Spirit connotes a depth of sensitivity that forms the matrix
of relations in which all life is cast. . . . We may say that spirit is a quality
of being which arises out of a particular depth of sensitivity in relations.
It is, in other words, a goodness in relationships."[3]

The doctrine of the Holy Spirit leads to the doctrine of the Trinity.
A brief discussion of the Trinity in process terms is important at this
point. According to theologians, there are two approaches to the Trinity: the *economic Trinity* and the *immanent Trinity*.[4] For our purposes,
these can be described as the Trinity as experienced by humans and the
Trinity as experienced by the Godhead. I accept the development of
the economic Trinity (from *oikomenos*, or God's relationship to humans
through the church) because of the witness of Christians through the
centuries. Most Christian believers pray to God, idealize the life and
witness of Jesus, and feel the presence of the Holy Spirit. God seems to
come to human life in three persons, because believers accept what the
church authorities have said, and because it fits their personal religious
imagination and experience. Most believers are not troubled by the doctrine of the Trinity as a description of God's presence in our lives.

The immanent Trinity is what some theologians call "ontological,"
that is, a doctrine that tries to describe in philosophical terms how God
can be three persons in unity and how these three persons relate to one
another outside of their relationships to humans. Questions of the immanent Trinity became important during the christological debates of the
early church councils around the status of Jesus. Was Jesus really God,
or was Jesus a superhuman being who became mediator between God

and humans? The early theologians decided that Jesus was of the same substance as God (and humans) but his own person. This made room for the Holy Spirit to become the third member of the Trinity, although the churches have never agreed on a precise doctrine of the Spirit. Most Christian believers have little interest or understanding of the immanent Trinity.

Most worship and Christian life ignores the Trinity in practice, so some theologians have questioned whether it is a functional doctrine. Recent feminist and process theology scholarship has brought some interesting perspectives that are helpful. As noted earlier, Whitehead's basic insight was identification of the relational process that underlies all of reality, "the many become one and are increased by one." In this insight the question of unity and multiplicity in the ongoing process of becoming is central. In the actual moment of experience, all things from the past come together to create a new moment of experience. As soon as a person decides what to make of this reality, he or she contributes that existence to the reality of the ongoing process. Everything comes together and increases in the same instant. So the relational question is this: How can people be together in harmony and beauty while dynamically moving toward a novel future?

Catherine LaCugna argues that the doctrine of the Trinity is the basis for a relational view of reality. Just as God, Jesus, and the Spirit are mutually interrelated with equality and empowerment, so humans can be related in the same way. The distortions of hierarchy, inequality, and domination are not valid forms of reality, but a result of human sin and evil.[5] Kathryn Tanner argues that the core value of the Trinity is generosity in which the three persons give to one another without being diminished themselves. This is especially important in contrast to a capitalist economy where humans compete for scarce goods so that a gain for one is a loss for others. This competitive aggressive system of thought and action is the basis for most human violence. But the Trinity offers an alternative conception of mutual empowerment through generosity so that an increase in value for one person is an increase in value for everyone else because the full community is enriched to everyone's benefit.[6]

What is the work and character of the Holy Spirit?

Understanding the Holy Spirit as a sign of the grace-filled generosity of God who relates to us in love rather than jealousy and judgment appeals to many believers and provides the basis for relational hope. What are the implications of such a view of divine Trinity for the church?[7]

CHURCHES AS THE BODY OF CHRIST

I believe the Church is called to be the body of Christ, a community of bodies and spirits, of humans and nature, in communion with the Holy Spirit.[8]

God is faithful; by God you were called into the fellowship [*koinonia*] of God's son, Jesus Christ our Lord. (1 Cor. 1:9)

God is spirit. [Humans], created in God's image, [have] spiritual existence, not as something added to [their] bodily substance, but as the expression of that concrete *body-mind unity* which [they are as persons]. The freedom of spirit is the freedom of God as the ultimate form-giving and life-giving reality. The freedom of [human beings] is also the freedom of spirit, but within the conditions of finite existence.[9]

Christians, the community of those who confess Christ and follow Jesus in their lives, have been called into the *koinonia*, the economy or household of Jesus Christ. Being a Christian means choosing to value the whole relational web that was created by God. Choosing nonviolence toward the relational web is a decision about one's identity, since the web is torn by violence such as war, poverty, family abuse, and ecological disaster. Choosing economic justice within the relational web means practicing values that are inclusive and move toward equality for all humans and nature.

All humans exist within the web of relationships that includes the natural creation. Our bodies are constantly recycling oxygen, carbon dioxide, water, and food in continual interaction with the atmosphere, the mineral world, the surface of the earth, and the animal and plant worlds. The theological traditions that overemphasize human life at the expense of the natural world have resulted in violence and exploitation of nature. Our search for nonviolence and economic justice must include the community of humans and nature.[10]

Linda and Philip, discussed in previous chapters, form test cases for my doctrine of the church in this section. Linda found her voice as a survivor of violence on her pilgrimages to El Salvador, and she embarked on her healing journey with the accompaniment of her therapist and other Christian leaders who were in Christian ministry. I was privileged to be part of the extended network of support for her. Because of sexual abuse by her mother in a "Christian" home and sexual abuse by many men in the local community, Linda chose to leave the church as an active member. Philip was a seminary student when he abused two adolescent boys in his role as a public school counselor. He pled guilty and served eight years in prison and was stig- What narratives from con-matized as a sex offender with all temporary life give you of the restrictions. Even though he insight into the nature of the hungered for a church that could church? accompany him on his journey toward healing, he felt endangered by harsh judgments or denial and easy forgiveness. He has not been able to find a church where he can be himself with all his multiplicity and ambiguity.

One of the questions that guides this chapter is, What kind of church would be safe and challenging for Linda, a survivor of violence, and for Philip, a survivor and perpetrator of violence? As you will see in the following discussion, it is not easy to understand the depths of human sin and violence and respond with the full grace of God.

MARKS OF FAITHFUL CHURCHES

The following five marks of faithful churches grow out of the discussion of the Trinitarian God of previous chapters:

1. Inclusive Relationality

Both Linda and Philip need a community where they can be fully accepted and loved for who they are with all their gifts and limita-tions. In fact, this is what the church is called to be—a place where the oppressed and sinners can seek healing, redemption, and creative min-istries. Linda needs a community where victims/survivors can be safe, where her concerns are taken seriously, and where she can experience compassionate limits for her own emotional volatility. Philip needs a community where he can find support for his suffering and compassion-ate accountability for his abusive attitudes and behaviors.[11]

Process theology provides the basis for my understanding of how inclusive love is possible. In each moment of experience, we are shaped by the full reality of everything that has existed up to that point in history. The immediate past moment includes the whole material reality brought to focus in the immediate present. Love, in my understanding, is a quality of interaction characterized by sensitivity that moves toward communion with self, others, and God. That is, we are called to embrace the reality of the world we have inherited, valuing it for what it is, and seeking to harmonize the many contradictions and contrasts that are present there. In our emerging experience, we have no choice about receiving the effects of the past actual world. However, we do have choices about how to value this inheritance from the past.[12]

Given the power of the past to shape the actual occasion, there is a tendency to accept and continue the values of certain experiences. Since sexual abuse has been a taboo subject for many centuries, most communities are content to continue this taboo through silence and silencing. That is, we do not listen to the suffering of survivors and perpetrators, and we actively pressure them to keep silent so that our fantasy of peace and stability will not be disrupted. Since perpetrators of sexual abuse are increasingly stigmatized in our society, there is a tendency to conform to this value. It takes courage and insight to challenge this part of the past actual world and receive the full experience that Linda and Philip have to offer. Process theology describes the process that makes this receptivity possible.

> How do the churches practice the inclusive love of God?

The process theory of value suggests that beauty is the harmonization of the maximum depth and breadth of experience because it can produce unity with intensity. Bernard Loomer calls this "receptive power" or "size," by which he means "the range of intensity of relationships one can help create and sustain."[13] He believes that Jesus is a helpful figure because he was able to sustain the intensity of love and hate, life and death, into his being. Because of Jesus' life, death, and resurrection, we know that overcoming these contradictions is humanly possible, and we are empowered to follow Jesus by acting with courage to embody the contradictions of our generation. Linda and Philip represent contemporary limits of inclusive love for church and society.[14]

Accepting inclusive love as a goal of Christian life calls us to a radical reevaluation of ourselves and our communities. Linda and Philip need a community where they can be understood and accepted with all of their mixture of experiences.

2. Empowering Justice

Justice is the appropriate use of power to produce and distribute resources for the community. Linda and Philip are hypersensitive to uses and abuses of power. They have both experienced abuse and the denial of resources essential for integral human life. In addition, Philip knows the shame of his own abuse of power that was destructive of other vulnerable persons. Any community that is naïve about its own uses of power is a dangerous place for people like Linda and Philip. Justice includes safety and accountability. That is, a loving community is a safe place where people are not abused again and a place where abuse of power is confronted and dealt with compassionately and firmly. Where is the community that is sufficiently self-critical about its internal power structure and its location in the larger structures and ideologies of domination? Where is the community that understands the depths of its own sinful attempts to abuse power over others and responds with accountability to protect the vulnerable? The Presbyterian Church (USA) Book of Order has a good discussion of power and accountability in the church. Every member is given power to serve the church, and every member is accountable for that power to the authority of the church.[15] When this model of church is practiced, there is a possibility of greater justice in the world.

Process theology believes that there is a moment of irreducible freedom in each moment of experience that provides the possibility for novelty to emerge. Previously, I have said that creativity, the ability to respond to others with new feelings, is loving when it moves toward enlarged freedom for self, others, and God.[16] That is, accepting the past actual world and seeking new harmonies and intensities is a way of enlarging freedom for the whole web of creation. Our receptivity of the past actual world and our causal effects for the future means that we emerge from the exercise of the power of others and our decisions have power for future others. Both our receptivity and our decisions to shape the future are acts of power. We must choose in each moment how to receive the abuses of power from the past and whether to be abusive in the way we exercise power in the future. Because of our freedom, we have responsibility to examine our own complicity in abuse of power and find novel ways to transform these abuses into enlarged freedom for all.

When Jesus met Zacchaeus in the tree, Jesus knew who and what Zacchaeus was and did not ignore the justice issues in his life. Yet Jesus sensed that Zacchaeus was a man who was ready for a transformation. Jesus initiated a relationship with Zacchaeus that helped move him toward justice by sharing a meal in his home and giving him a new vision of how he could restore balance in his life through restitution toward those he had harmed. Jesus received Zacchaeus with all his ambiguity and helped him develop a new way of proceeding with his life that was not based on abuse of power.

> How can the churches exercise power as a witness to Jesus Christ?

Linda and Philip need a community characterized by loving justice in terms of power so that they can express their power safely for healing and human thriving, and so that they help all to recognize abuses of power in themselves and others. Process theology helps me to understand the positive and negative possibilities of power in human life, and helps me to see that power can be an expression of love.

3. Nonviolent Resistance to Evil

Linda and Philip have been victims of evil, and Philip has engaged in behaviors that he understands as evil. In both cases, evil has taken the form of violence and violation of the humanity of others by someone. In my own work I have defined evil as an abuse of power that destroys human bodies and spirits and the whole ecosystem. Genuine evil arises within the convergence of power in individual agency, social ideologies and institutions, and religious sanctions. When these systems of domination are established and perpetuated over generations and centuries, they develop into systems such as patriarchy, racism, and economic oppression. Such ideologies identify permanent populations of vulnerable people who regularly become victims of interpersonal violence.[17] Female children are especially vulnerable to sexual violence because their humanity is made ambiguous. African American gay men are vulnerable to victimization because of the history of racialized sexual stereotypes and practices.

In process theology, moments of experience inherit systems of domination from the past actual world. Occasions in the past have conformed to and in some cases actively perpetuated these oppressive systems. In some theologies, evil is defined by nonbeing.[18] But within process theology, evil systems bent on destruction are active forces that perpetuate themselves in an atmosphere of ignorance and apathy and unenlightened self-interest.[19] For example, many white people benefit by conforming to the ideologies and practices of racism and lack the courage to engage in active resistance that would disrupt their intimate networks and political and economic alliances. For generations, men have accommodated to ideologies and practices of sexism that devalue women and prevent them from expressing their full humanity. For members of the dominant classes, accommodation to evil systems limits the competition for economic benefits and leadership opportunities and creates permanent subordinate classes that can be exploited on many levels. It takes great effort to resist and challenge the power of such evil systems in one's own personal and community life.

Linda and Philip are both seeking a community of nonviolent resistance. They need intimate relationships that are attuned to the human problem of abuse of power and who know about systems of domination that institutionalize power in abusive ways. They have spent their lives facing evil in others and in themselves and, during the healing process, they have chosen nonviolent resistance to evil. They need a community that knows about personal, social, and religious evil and organizes its life around nonviolent resistance on all levels of their corporate life.

Within human experience, resistance to evil is a loving response to systems of domination. That is, in an emerging experience, persons can choose to minimize the effects of evil systems, can choose to be open to the witness of victims of these systems, and can identify with communities of resistance and appropriate their wisdom. Thus, there is a basis for resistance to evil within the ontology of process theology.

> How can the churches balance Jesus' call to nonviolence and Jesus' call to social justice?

I call this mark of community "nonviolent resistance to evil" because the use of violence to fight against evil creates a mimetic system that inevitably becomes corrupt and abusive. That is, many revolutions are based on the same consciousness and abuse of power as the systems they replace. With the help of Ched Myers,[20] I see in Jesus' teaching of the disciples an alternative vision. While the disciples were attracted to Jesus' critique of the religious and political leadership and his empowerment of the poor, they were slow to understand the new vision of nonviolent power he was teaching. Jesus tried to teach them alternative images such as servanthood and friendship. He engaged in rituals such as the foot washing in John 13 and the ritual of bread and wine in the upper room. In some ways the crucifixion itself was a kind of radical teaching that nonviolent resistance to the point of death is sometimes the necessary path to expose the corrupt violence of evil systems.

I was twenty-five years old when Martin Luther King was assassinated on April 4, 1968. His murder radicalized me because I realized that there is no limit to what human beings will do to maintain their dominant position in society. King is a christological figure for me and shows me the possibilities and the risks of nonviolent resistance to evil. Any community that responds to the victims and perpetrators of violence must understand the possible value and cost of nonviolent resistance to evil.

Loomer reminds us that good and evil are embedded in the same energy—the rhythm of sensitivity to past experiences and creative exercise of our personal freedom. Therefore, evil within a person or community cannot be destroyed without also destroying the good.[21] Good and evil can be harmonized only within a larger event. Resistance to evil is a useful image because it reminds us that the possibilities of relative good and evil are always part of our decisions. We cannot avoid this ambiguity because every decision will be a mixture of good and evil. But we can cultivate a discipline of resistance by knowing that evil is always a possibility. In every moment we live on a razor's edge between good and evil, and there is no other place to live without falling into evil itself.

Nonviolent resistance was a part of my childhood training. It was defined as an active, forceful engagement in justice work with a commitment to minimizing the violence in our personal lives. Responding to Linda and Philip as persons is more than passive receptivity. They have lived in hell, and they demand real engagement from everyone who takes them seriously. They are hypersensitive to power and control. They know when someone is trying to exercise power over them. In Emmanuel Lévinas's terms, they know that they represent an irreducible otherness for most people, and they will accept nothing less than active engagement without any residue of violation of their humanity.[22] Both Linda and Philip can intuitively sense hypocrisy, paternalism, and condescension in any relationship. They quickly abandon hope if they sense that someone is not willing to be vulnerable and affected by who they are. Given the vulnerability of their lives, they have no time for additional violence, and they want to know if you are an ally in their nonviolent resistance to evil. In process theology terms, Linda and Philip are acutely aware of the contradictions in their own lives. They seek partners in finding harmony for these contradictions. But they demand nothing less than partners who are also willing to examine their own contradictions and seek a greater harmony. Local churches that already have everything worked out are dangerous places for them because there is too little active resistance to evil.

4. Multiplicity and Unity

Linda and Philip represent forms of multiplicity that have not yet been harmonized in U.S. church and society. Within the United States, many people are more hospitable toward victims of sexual violence than they were thirty years ago, but we still have a long way to go. We have only just begun to deal with the issues raised by sex offenders in our communities. Linda and Philip represent many thousands who are victims and perpetrators of sexual and other forms of interpersonal violence. Their existence as political subjects is a recent social construction. In previous generations, victims were expected to be silent about their experiences, otherwise they would be rejected, stigmatized, and marginalized. Abusers were protected if they had social status, but often scapegoated if they came from unprotected social groups. Society has taken a first step toward greater safety and accountability by identifying the widespread reality of sexual violence.

Creativity means that God is creating ever-new multiplicities that challenge particular visions of human life.[23] Whenever human community becomes comfortable with its level of harmony and intensity, we need to know that God has already created new multiplicities that will threaten that comfort. From a human point of view, this means that the true God is always experienced by humans as multiple.

A possible implication of this endemic multiplicity is that God in Godself is defined by multiplicity. Theology has a long debate about the multiplicity and unity of God. Within process theology we have the debate between the rational/speculative and empirical wings. I agree with the rational wing that we need nonanalogical ways of speaking about God so that we can conceive of God at all, such as the primordial and consequent natures (primordial refers to God's unchanging nature; consequent refers to the part of God that is changed by relationships with the creation). But my personal disposition is to agree with the empirical wing of process theology that God's consequent nature has particular importance for human beings because it is the part of God that changes and therefore is fully relational.[24] The consequent nature of God is characterized by multiplicity because the world is multiple, and this provides a foundation for thinking about the precarious balance of multiplicity and unity in human efforts to construct beauty.

I believe Linda and Philip represent a new multiplicity that is coming into public focus. Linda has survived one of the worst kinds of violence a human being can face—a deliberate attempt by her mother to deform and destroy her bodily and spiritual integrity as a person. Many times, Linda was sure that her mother would kill her; yet she survived. Even when doctors examined her and identified her as an abused child, they returned her to her parents for further abuse. Her suffering was ignored because of the sin of her parents and the social ideologies of gender, class, and family privacy. Philip is the survivor of centuries of oppression and dehumanization that have been directed at African Americans, at African American men, at

How can the churches witness to God's love of multiplicity and also strive for the unity Jesus prayed for?

African American sexuality, and at homosexuals. His crimes against two African American adolescents perpetuated these forms of violence at several levels. His imprisonment represents one of many forms of violence imposed on men of color in the United States out of proportion to their crimes.[25]

Linda and Philip represent a public voice for a new kind of multiplicity, not because such human experiences have never existed in history before, but because the courageous witness of survivors and the
feminist movement in Western nations has forced many societies to
address these complex issues. Loomer says that God (or creativity) is
a multiplicity seeking unity. He says that there is little evidence that
such unity has been achieved. If we follow Loomer and use an empirical
method that counts as evidence only what we conceive as true in this
embodied process of being human, how can we understand the world
except as a multiplicity?[26] Some days, there is very little evidence that
this multiplicity is seeking unity. In any case, the challenge to church
and society today is how to accept the reality of the actual multiplicity
that we have in ourselves, in others, and in God, and how to continue
to live with courage toward the greater unity that is possible. The ability
to have moments of relative unity given this multiplicity is the potential
beauty that Whitehead posited. I am seeking to understand the church
as a community of multiplicity and unity where Linda and Philip could
be full members with their multiplicity.

5. Ambiguity and Goodness

Linda and Philip are both ambiguous figures. On the one hand, they
are clearly victims of multiple systems of violence and domination. On
the other hand, they live with enormous amounts of ambivalence about
themselves, others, and God. Neither one is willing to settle for the
respectable, numbing, middle-class life within the United States. The
compromises to their integrity are too great. They help me remember
that neither should I be comfortable living in U.S. culture. The ambiguity of their lives and mine is internal and external and cannot be
eradicated.

Loomer said that ambiguity must be a metaphysical category.[27] If
we accept a relational/process worldview, then there is no way to resolve
the ambiguity of good and evil in the actual world, and there is no way
to live comfortably with the ambiguity. We are caught in a permanent
muddle[28] that has no easy resolution but within which the search for
goodness is our lifeline to the future. God is as much a part of this ambiguity as we are. God, according to Bernard Loomer, is implicated in the
full history of the world. As the Hebrew Bible testifies, many of God's

projects have not worked out well—the flood in Genesis, the kings of Israel, the exile and its consequences, the crucifixion of Jesus. The consequences of God's actions in human history are ambiguous.

I see no way to escape this terrible ambiguity, especially since I have learned the hard way that the muddle of ambiguity is the very source of my creativity and love and goodness. I try to seek the good in everything I do, but I already know that the beginning and end of my endeavors will be ambiguous. Linda cannot undo the sexual abuse by her mother and the lifelong consequences of fragility that have followed. Philip cannot undo the fact that he turned from victim to perpetrator and damaged the lives of two young African American boys. Freud believed that the binary opposition of good and evil in infancy was a developmental stage on the way to maturity and acceptance of what he called "ambivalence," by which he meant the irreducible mixture of love and hate toward the primary persons in one's life and object world. In the same way, I believe that ambiguity is an advance in theological anthropology and doctrine of God over the binary emphasis on omnipotence and perfection. We need a God who is competent and ambiguous, and I yearn for the day when we can understand Jesus in this way. Where is the community that does not need categories of God and humanity that are pure, but can understand that the tension of ambiguity and goodness is often an increase in value over purity?

> Does the ambiguity of the churches express or contradict their witness to Jesus Christ?

SUMMARY

In this chapter I have described five marks that I believe are norms for the faithful Christian Church based on Scripture, systematic theology, and personal religious experience. In the next chapter I describe some of the practices that I believe follow from these principles. In summary, I believe that the church is the living body of Christ, the material and spiritual embodiment of Jesus who lived, died, and was resurrected in the first century C.E. It is the mission of the church to be faithful to the vision we learn from Jesus Christ, and to fulfill the mission of God through the power of the Holy Spirit. How do we know when we are being faithful? We need practical norms that can guide us when we make material decisions about our individual, corporate, and religious lives. These norms themselves stand under the judgment of the triune God, and doubtless new generations of Christians will find new ways of understanding and articulating these norms. But human beings cannot live without norms by which they organize their perceptions and make their decisions as they receive and create power in the world.

I believe the church is called to embody inclusive love, empowering justice, nonviolent resistance to evil, multiplicity and unity, and ambiguity and goodness. Whether the particular mission of a congregation is to accompany survivors and perpetrators of domestic violence, witness against the corruption of global capitalism, maintain radical openness to intercultural and inter-religious experiences, or resist the destruction of the global environment, the faithful church will adhere to these five norms. Through rituals of liturgy and sacraments, education and care, evangelism and social justice, local congregations can re-present to the community of believers and the larger community the vision of a resilient, ambiguous God whose radical love and power redeems the world from its own destruction and offers the promise of transformation and new life.

How do the five marks of the church in this chapter correspond to the classical marks of the church: one, holy, catholic, and apostolic?

SIX
Eschatology:
Theologies of Hope

I believe in the eschaton, the telos of God's love and power, as an image of a harmonious community of peace and prosperity for all human and nonhuman beings including the material world. The ritual saying, "Christ will come again," means that all creation groans for the beloved community that God intends. Jesus comes through the Spirit in every moment that the love and power of God are fully disclosed in reality. The hope for Jesus' coming in the future is a lure toward the harmony and beauty given by God for all creation.

What can Christians hope for? What is the end toward which God's love and power aim? *Eschaton* is a Greek word meaning last things—the telos (end or goal) toward which God is moving the creation. Marjorie Suchocki defines hope as the process of creative transformation through Christ that is at work in human life:

> The amazing hope that is offered by viewing Christ as the principle of creative transformation is not simply that God is at work in human history, working in us, with us, and through us, for the incarnation of peace, but that the peace that so draws us is not illusory. It is grounded in the very nature of God and is mediated to us in every [moment of life].[1]

God's love and power aims toward a new earth in which all people and the earth live together in peace and harmony, a community of togetherness that preserves our multiplicity and ambiguity and overcomes our contradictions for the sake of beauty. Christians follow Christ because, as humans, we hope for the peaceful and harmonious world that God intends. Our hope is beyond our imagination, so we trust in God to lead us into a future that we cannot yet see.

In process theology, what happens on earth among human beings, animals, plants, and the nonbiological world is critical to God's telos. When there is an end to life on earth, which will surely come, its beauty will be preserved. Until the end, God calls us to live courageously with inclusive love, empowering justice, nonviolence resistance to evil, multiplicity and unity, and ambiguity and goodness.

> What can Christians hope for? What is the end toward which God's love and power aim?

The assumption of my project is that God exists and is an active part of the spiritual and material reality that human beings know as everyday life. God not only cares what happens to human beings and all creation, but God also is involved in mutual relationships with the same realities we know. This means that the everyday suffering and hope that we have in our lives interacts with God's suffering and hope.

How does a Christian "keep hope alive"[2] in the face of the accumulation of human evil in the twenty-first century? The list of dangers at every level of social and personal life is alarming:

- The rates of violence against women are epidemic.

- The rates of family violence, including the sexual abuse of children, continue in ever-new forms.

- The United States has invaded and initiated military action in dozens of countries since 1945 in order to establish its global economic empire.

- Local cultures, languages, and religions are endangered by systems of domination with the resulting loss of particular ways of perceiving, thinking, and feeling.

- Environmental disaster looms on every side—global warming, species extinction, monocultural agriculture with genetic modifications, water contamination, exploding human population, and so forth.

- More people suffer under the oppression of poverty than ever before and this population grows unchecked.

- Global capitalism has failed as a strategy for creating democratic governments and economic abundance.

- Christian churches compete with one another and with non-Christian religious groups for hegemony in the world.

There is room for pessimism today, and many progressive Christians have become discouraged and personally depressed. I was born in 1942 during the most violent time in the history of humanity. More people were killed between 1942 and 1945 than at any other comparable time in human history. Hitler's killing camps in Auschwitz and fifteen thousand other camps were operating at full capacity until the end of World War II and twelve million people were killed in the camps; more millions of people were murdered by the German military machine. At the same time, the Japanese were engaged in concentration camps and massacres in China, Korea, Indonesia, and other countries in East and Southeast Asia. In Nanjing, China, in 1937, 300,000 people were killed in six weeks.[3] Thousands of people in eastern and southern Asia were starved to death, worked to death, or died of preventable diseases because there was little food and medical care during the war. Meanwhile, the German army was attacking Moscow and laying waste to the populated areas in western Russia. By the end of the war, twenty million Russian citizens would be killed, the biggest loss of any nation during the war. The United States responded to Germany with saturation bombing of German cities, killing tens of thousands in Dresden, Hamburg, and other cities. At the end of the war, the United States became the only nation in history to drop nuclear bombs on populated areas; in Hiroshima and Nagasaki, 750,000 people were killed with two bombs. All in all, fifty million people were killed from the beginning to the end of WWII, from 1933 through 1945.

What are the obstacles to hope in your experience?

Twentieth-century Western theology responded to the depravity of the Holocaust and the war, deepened their understandings of sin and evil, and looked for new sources of hope. During the postwar decades, the world was in traumatic shock, though some remember the 1950s in the United States as an ideal time of peace and prosperity.

The 1960s brought a dramatic turn toward idealism through the civil rights and peace movements. The leaders in these two movements were impressed with the economic and political recovery of the Western world since WWII and believed that justice and prosperity could be extended to all people. The most far-reaching ideas came from the African American community, led by soldiers returning from European and Asian battlefields who refused to accept segregation and poverty for the African American community. Starting immediately after the war, African American groups energized ongoing historical resistance to segregation in schools and public facilities, eventually winning drastic changes in laws and local habits in the southern United States.

At the height of the civil rights movement, the war in Vietnam became a hot political issue. The same ideology and strategies that the reform movements used to challenge segregation and white supremacy were directed against the political decision to intervene in a poor country twelve thousand miles away. The analysis of the peace movement revealed that the war had less to do with national security and more to do with global strategies for United States' domination of other countries. The years 1965 through 1972 were a hopeful time for my generation because we believed that a more just world was possible and we were willing to work and sacrifice to make it happen.

Signs that our idealism was misplaced began to appear early, however, in a series of political assassinations: President John Kennedy (1963), Malcolm X (1965), Martin Luther King Jr. (1968), and presidential candidate Robert Kennedy (1968). Riots in larger northern urban centers disturbed our belief that the change could be won nonviolently. The killing of four students at a Kent State peace demonstration in 1972 was a blow to the peace movement.

The idealistic hope of the 1960s was replaced by deep despair in many persons in my generation. There appeared to be no limit to the greed and violence of persons with economic and political power in their quest to increase their power and wealth. Corporations regularly make decisions that cost the lives and health of millions of people and, when confronted, they deny the reality, deny responsibility, and deny restitution for the victims. One of the most egregious examples is the tobacco industry, which deliberately makes a product that kills people, markets it as a form of personal pleasure, and usually opposes all attempts by the government to address the public health issues. There are many corporations in the agricultural and food industries, health care and pharmaceutical industries, and those who manufacture military hardware and guns who are willing to sacrifice millions of people for economic and political benefits for a small group of people. The proliferation of guns and military weapons around

the world is a crime against human-
ity. The current economic crisis | What are the signs of hope in
caused by greed and corruption in | your experience?
banks and financial institutions is the
latest example of systematic human
evil with great cost to the people of the world. In 2010, British Petroleum,
Halliburton, and Transocean corporations polluted the Gulf of Mexico
with oil by shortchanging safety requirements in favor of profit. The full
impact of this ecological catastrophe will affect many generations.

WHERE IS THE HOPE?

My hope lies in the resilient love and power of the trinitarian God and
the history of courageous witnesses over the centuries.[4] The movement
to prevent violence against women arose out of the feminist analysis of
the personal experiences of women, including the violence that infects
families and intimate relationships. Among other things, the feminist
movement focused on partner battering and murder and sexual abuse of
women and children. Through a combination of social analysis and psychological theories of trauma and healing, politicized activists organized
to prevent violence and provide healing for survivors. I became a recruit
and then an advocate for prevention of interpersonal violence through
this new movement. For my own sense of hope, I depend particularly on
my relationships with survivors of violence. I see evidence of hope in the
resilience of survivors of violence I have been privileged to know, and in
the many activists all over the world who are concerned about economic
justice, peace, and ecological balance.

Many of the survivors I know were not supposed to survive—someone tried to kill their bodies and spirits. Yet they did survive, and their
witness is miraculous because so many victims of violence do not survive.
The ones who survive show great courage, and they show that survival is
possible for the human spirit. I believe that human beings have a possibility of a resilient spirit after violence because of the love and power of God.

I have seen glimpses of hope in some abusers I have known well. After
perpetrating the sexual abuse of a child, how does one recover a sense of
integrity and empathy for self and others? I have seen abusers look at themselves with courage and honesty and seek life and healthy relationships. I

believe that human beings are capable of examining the deepest sin and evil in themselves and finding their way back into humanity because of the resilient love and power of God.

I am encouraged by the many grassroots social movements working to protect the environment, provide resources for survivors of violence, challenge corporations that cause global poverty, and take on the military machines of every nation.

Where do you find the courageous witness of survivors of evil to the power of God's love in history?

Empires come and go, but they have never completely destroyed the human and divine spirits of compassion in the world.

STRATEGIES OF HOPE

Jesus lived in a time of great danger, and the people of Galilee were faced with several strategies for responding to their oppression:

1. to accommodate to the current authorities and try to survive until a better day;

2. to work for reforms that would make things better;

3. to survive the present situation whatever it took;

4. to rebel and try to overthrow the authorities;[5]

5. to withdraw from public life and try to maintain certain values for the future.

It is possible to find Christians who have chosen each of these options today, and from time to time, most of us are attracted to all of these options at one time or another. I can personally understand the logic of all of these positions, and have practiced all of them in one way or another. Each position has its own logic of hope.

Accommodation

Those who accommodate look at the long-term future and believe the community will survive. They see that difficult crises have come and gone over the centuries. Some crises are harder than others, and there is more danger at one time than another, but they believe that just as the community has survived hard times before, they will survive these times. There is confidence that the community is tough and will survive. The Jews survived persecution in Europe for many centuries; they always managed to outlast their oppressors and regained relative freedom to practice their historic faith. Making compromises with the oppressive powers is sometimes the only way to survive until another day when the community is free to set its own agenda. The Sadducees believed that accommodation with the Romans was necessary so that the Temple rituals could be maintained.[6] They were willing to make compromises with the Romans in exchange for a limited religious freedom. The regular pilgrimage of people to Jerusalem shows the power of the Temple as a symbol of Jewish identity.

However, accommodation also has its dangers. How does the community know how corporate identity will be affected by the compromises that are made with dominating powers? Will the people be able to sustain their faith despite the time of persecution? One weakness of accommodation is that this time the threats to survival may be different, because survival is not inevitable. Accommodation did not protect Israel from becoming slaves in Egypt, or from suffering desolation during captivity in Babylon. The decades of accommodation did not protect the Temple from destruction in 68 C.E., nor did it prevent the Roman violence directed to the people who lived in Palestine. In Germany in 1933 some leaders of the European Jewish community believed that the Nazi persecutions were just another in a series of pogroms over many centuries. Every few decades Christians persecuted the Jewish community to avoid facing their own issues. Even though many people were killed in past pogroms, the community itself survived. But for European Jews in Germany, this time was different. By the end of the war 80 to 90 percent of the Jewish people in Germany and Poland, including rabbis and other intellectuals, were killed, ending forever certain forms of Judaism. Jewish theologians proclaim that Judaism was forever changed by the Holocaust and the impact of these changes is being worked through today with many different forms of Judaism proclaiming the true identity of the historic faith.

Reform

Those who call for reform evaluate the current crisis as an opportunity to make significant changes that will help the community to survive.

The Pharisees called for the development of local synagogues and the decentralization of authority so that more people could participate in the religious rituals and laws.[7] The synagogue system became one of the survival mechanism after 70 C.E. While the reform did not prevent the violence of 68–70 C.E., these synagogues did equip the survivors with tools that enabled the Jews to reorganize after the end of the Temple-centered faith. Frederick Douglas and Martin Luther King Jr. were reformers in their own times, each calling for a change in strategy in the African American community and demanding a change in laws and practices in the dominant white community. The end of slavery and voting rights for African

What kind of social reform is faithful for the church in your community?

American men was a reform that changed the United States. Likewise, reform movements led to the end of school segregation and the open accommodations in many levels of U.S. society. Douglas and King are celebrated as heroes by later generations for correctly naming the crises and the possibilities for change under difficult conditions.

Survival

Most people in times of oppression adapt to the circumstances of their lives and do the best they can at as individuals and families to survive. Unless there is an effective movement that shows a real chance of changing the situation, most people do what they have to do to make it. Jeremiah bought a field in Israel just before the Babylonian Captivity because it symbolized the hope that someday the Jews would live here again, farm the land, marry and have children, and preserve the Jewish faith (Jeremiah 32). In Jesus' time, the Galilean farmers who lost their land did whatever they could to survive. Even though they shared hostility toward Rome and Jerusalem, their day-to-day struggle dominated their time and energy. Emil Fackenheim advocates a new Jewish law of survival in response to the Holocaust. He argues that those who survived the Holocaust were resisting evil and that we are commanded to remember their survival and honor what they did to survive.[8]

I think of the slaves during the eighteenth and early nineteenth centuries in the United States, when the institution of slavery was firmly established and supported by the government and the majority white population so that there was virtually no chance of reform or revolution in the short term. Delores Williams says that survival was an appropriate goal for the enslaved community and should be seen as a form of resistance to tyranny.[9]

When the Soviet Union was finally disolved in 1991, there was a remarkable resurgence of participation in the churches in the Republic of Russia. Empty churches filled up, and a new generation believed that the church had saved the best of Russian culture. The Russian grandmothers remembered their Christian faith and taught their grandchildren in the privacy of the home. In a system that places no value on the oppressed group and has no concern whether any individual lives or dies, survival is a way of beating the odds and living for another generation, thus defeating the intention of the oppressors.

> How can we have compassion for ourselves and others when survival seems like the only strategy of faithfulness?

Revolt

Those who call for revolt and revolution believe the oppression of the people is unbearable, and that the only way to respond to tyranny is to fight back. If the rebels organize and train themselves for military action, they might catch the empire in a weak moment, and if other revolts spring up in other parts of the empire, then perhaps overthrow of the corrupt authorities will be possible and a new nation can be developed. All empires eventually collapse when the people become unmanageable.

> Do you sometimes have sympathies with those who call for radical social change even if it requires violence?

Even if one particular revolt does not succeed, it contributes to the idea that empire is not inevitable and gives hope to the people. During times of oppression, there will always be calls for violent revolt and revolution. In the first century C.E., the Zealots challenged the Roman Empire and succeeded several times in liberating the Temple from the oppressor's control. The American Revolution of 1776 succeeded when the English Empire conceded defeat. Out of the revolution came a new nation with new principles.

The weakness of the revolutionary position is that military revolt can bring down even harsher persecution on the people as the empire takes revenge on the whole population for the violence of a few groups. When the Zealots of New Testament time took over the Temple in Jerusalem in 68 C.E., the Roman Empire was not vulnerable. The Imperial Army crushed the rebellion, destroyed the Temple, and massacred many Jews in Palestine. There were dozens of slave revolts in the United States during the eighteenth and nineteenth centuries, all of which were brutally put down and hundreds of people killed in revenge by white mobs. While these revolts themselves were not successful, they challenged the ideology that Africans were happy with the institution of slavery. Vincent Harding reports on the National Black Convention in 1854 when Martin Delany called for revolutionary action by all African Americans.[10] Study of the slave revolts and black nationalist movements is now a source of pride for scholars and students of history. Even Mahatma Gandhi preferred violent resistance to acceptance of oppression:

> Gandhi pointed out three possible responses to oppression and injustice. One he described as the coward's way: to accept the wrong or run away from it. The second option was to stand and fight by force of arms. Gandhi said this was *better* than acceptance or running away. But the *third* way, he said, was best of all and required the most courage: to stand and fight solely by nonviolent means.[11]

Withdrawal

Finally, some communities withdraw into separate communities to preserve certain precious values because they believe that even worse things will come to pass. The community needs to preserve the texts, rituals, and ideas for humanity in the future, and for the coming life in heaven. Such communities often develop apocalyptic ideologies about the end of history. Eventually the empire will collapse. When this happens, it is important for a faithful remnant to survive and carry on. The Essenes withdrew into caves during the first century C.E., and some of the texts they preserved have been invaluable for modern scholars trying to understand the Septuagint and the Christian New Testament. Separatist groups produced some of the most important apocalyptic literature that attacked the oppressor in symbolic language designed to give hope to the people (Daniel, Mark 13, Revelation). The Irish monks withdrew during the most difficult times in European history and some give them credit for preserving the New Testament because nearly all other copies were destroyed in the European violence. Certain utopian communities such as Hutterites, Amish, Bruderhof, and other groups in the United States have preserved ways of thinking that have great interest for those

who look for models of communities that survive without modern technology during the present ecological crises. In the twenty-first century some ecological communities have withdrawn into the wilderness to test the human will to survive the destruction of the planet. Some modern science fiction explores the survival of underground human communities in a time when robots take over the world through violence and mind control. It is possible for the human imagination to construct a rationale for withdrawal under extreme circumstances.

Does withdrawal into a utopian community sometimes appeal to you?

The weakness of the withdrawal position is that the community too often becomes isolated, missing opportunities to influence the world for good, and eventually becoming self-destructive. There are many examples of how separatist communities become authoritarian cults where open debate is punished and vulnerable people are abused by those with more power. Fear of apocalypse is a virulent tool for tyrants who desire control over other people.

* * * *

I believe that whenever communities are under conditions of oppression and tyranny, all five of these possibilities will be represented. In extreme circumstances such as Jews under Roman occupation, the groups will separate and take on institutional form, even considering other options to be betrayals of the group's identity. One group of Zealots called the Sacarii chose as their particular mission assassination of Jewish leaders they thought were collaborating with the oppressors. The Sacarii tried to undermine accommodation as an option in order to radicalize the population and prepare them for the military confrontation that was coming.

They reasoned that if accommodation failed, then revolt and revolution were left as the only realistic options.[12] The same phenomenon occurred in Poland in 1945 when the resistance fighters who fought against the Nazis later turned their guns on the Polish leaders who were collaborating with the Russian occupation. They reasoned that if these Polish leaders were killed, then the whole population would rise up against Russian tyranny.[13] We see the same phenomenon today in Iraq when Shiite gunman have killed off the Shiite religious leaders who cooperated with the U.S. occupation of their country even though the Shiite people controlled the primary institutions of the government. These are examples of religiously inspired military revolt against tyranny.

What this discussion shows is that the strategies for a hopeful future will depend on a community's understanding of its sociopolitical situation. Does the religious community believe that it lives under a tyranny that oppresses the people and their religious expressions? How severe is that oppression? Does the oppression threaten the identity and survival of the community and its religious beliefs? What are the most faithful and effective strategies for survival and liberation within this context? How shall the community practice its faith within this context? Religious communities have responded in various ways to these questions.

Ched Myers believes that Jesus represents an alternative to these five strategies for resisting systemic evil, an alternative he calls "alienated, confrontative, and nonaligned."[14] He suggests that the peasant farmers in Galilee were alienated from the Temple leaders in Jerusalem, sympathetic to the Zealots, and confrontational in their politics, but not convinced of the rebels' violent strategies. Myers asks: "What if a prophet arose who advocated a strategy that disdained Qumranite withdrawal *and* Pharisaic activism on the grounds that neither addressed the roots of oppression in the dominant social order?"[15] Myers suggests that the Gospel of Mark presents Jesus as such a prophet: "Though sympathetic to the socio-economic and political grievances of the rebels, Mark was compelled to repudiate their call to a defense of Jerusalem . . . because . . . the means (military) and ends (restorationist) of the 'liberation' struggle were fundamentally counterrevolutionary."[16]

> What sociopolitical signs give us clues about the nature of faithful practice in the world and its multiple crises?

Jesus was labeled a reformer, but he was too radical for the kinds of reforms that the Pharisees represented. Jesus was labeled a Zealot, but he was nonviolent in his strategy and did not believe that overthrow of the government would lead to a genuine revolution. Catherine Keller warns against "a condition of chronic moral indignation" that opposes the dominant symbolic order but still understands the world only in terms of power. She warns against both "imperialist messianism" and "revolutionary messianism" because they are mirror images of one another, still based on a false notion of power politics.[17]

> Is it possible for a citizen of a nation to be alienated, confrontative, and nonaligned?

Myers suggests that Jesus introduced a new way to respond to oppression, one that understands that systems of evil are based on violence. The Jesus way aims to destabilize systems of dominance and violence through nonviolent resistance and direct action. It is active, political, and potentially powerful. But its roots are in a "theopolitics" based on interdependent relationships and a different vision of hope. In the following section, I try to identify the empirical signs of hope that a new theopolitics[18] is already a part of our history and future.

A THEOPOLITICS OF HOPE

For me as a progressive-Anabaptist-Pietist Christian, what are the signs of hope, and what strategies are appropriate for this particular time? What does it mean in the twenty-first century to be "alienated, confrontative, nonaligned?"[19] I ask this question because I believe that many U.S. Christians with liberal backgrounds find themselves in this situation. At the beginning of the chapter I listed some of the issues of concern that many people share. Here I identify some of the social movements that inspire my hope and enliven my faith in Jesus Christ.

First, I am hopeful because of the women's movement of the last two centuries, which has identified the systemic problem of gender justice, particularly discrimination against women in leadership and violence against women such as sexual and domestic violence. I am inspired by the many prophetic leaders who have emerged to give a comprehensive analysis of patriarchy. The women's movement has many different strategies from accommodationist to reform to separatism to revolt.

Powerful forces are committed to maintaining the traditional gender hierarchies of men over women—anti-abortion groups, anti-divorce groups, fathers' rights groups, family values groups, abstinence groups, pro-marriage groups, and so forth. There has been a resurgence of global backlash against gender justice movements as illustrated by Roman Catholic rejection of women's ordination, Sharia laws in Islam, dowry laws in India, and trafficking in women in Asia, Latin America, and Africa. In response to these challenges, some women have become conservative in their views and have been rewarded with political power. Phyllis Schlafly, Beverly LaHaye, Lynne Cheney, Sarah Palin, and other women have gained power by supporting traditional gender hierarchies. Paradoxically, these women show that the limitations placed on women as a social class make no sense since they have each achieved national and global leadership as women.

Some women have dedicated themselves to reforms, becoming lawyers, politicians, doctors, lawyers, scientists, and ministers in order to sustain the movement toward gender justice. They have shown that there are no essential limitations to leadership because of gender. Some women have focused on their individual achievements assuming that the necessary changes have already been made. A few women have engaged in revolt by shooting their abusive male partners. A group of women have sought solace in Wicca, Asian, and New Age religious experiences with other women in a separatist mode. I believe that the women's movement is of God and that its long-term effects will be positive and revolutionary for culture, religion, institutions, and interpersonal relationships. I believe that men can be profeminist, understanding themselves as allies of the women's movement and taking their clues for strategy from wise women they trust. The women's movement gives me hope in the future.

Second, and closely related to the women's movement is the movement for liberation of gay, lesbian, bisexual, transgendered, intersexual, and queer persons (sometimes referred to as the GLBTIQ movement). For many decades, initiated by individual activists and organized into a political movement after the Stonewall revolt of 1968,[20] the resistance movement of nonheterosexual persons has challenged the dominance of the narrow theologies and ethics that limit sexual identity and behavior to heterosexual relationships. This movement has shown that heterosexism is a social construction that does great harm to the whole community by pre-scribing rigid gender roles and alien forms of human desire. The GLTBIQ movement promises to transform the personal identities of all persons in the direction of God's intentions for human life.

Third, I am hopeful because of the global movements for eco-nomic justice. Through my travels across the United States, Europe, Nicaragua, Korea, and Ghana, I have seen nonaligned agencies (called NGOs, nongovernmental organizations), who have amazingly creative responses to the global economy. They fund and support many grass-roots organizations to empower local people in their struggle for survival and integrity. From these same groups comes a prophetic critique of global capitalism that shows up in reformers and protesters at meetings of global economic power. I have reviewed some of these projects in my book, *Render Unto God*.[21]

The relative and absolute poverty in the world has increased in the last thirty years in spite of the promises of the International Monetary Fund, the World Bank, and the World Trade Organization. Many Chris-tians who supported the so-called Bretton Woods institutions[22] in the early days have become discouraged by the failure of these institutions to curb poverty and environmental disaster.[23] Instead, it appears that the effect of these economic projects has been the consolidation of power and wealth in the hands of a few people in the wealthiest nations at the expense of everyone else. Hundreds of millions of people are expendable in the programs of the new global economy. In response to this crisis, Christian progressives have lined up in all five of the positions described above. Some have joined the systems of power hoping to help them work for justice. Many more have joined NGOs with a focus of reform-ing the institutions of power that determine the extent of global pov-erty. Most concerned middle-class U.S. Christians have been passive in their actions and focused instead on surviving within their social status, grateful when their own health-care and pension plans have grown, fear-ful during times of recession. A few Christians have joined forces with the violent revolutions. For example, many progressive Christians in the United States have supported the Cuban revolution, the Sandinista revolution in Nicaragua, and the Vietnamese revolution to overthrow Western economic tyranny in favor of socialist alternatives. There have been some utopian experiments where people have tried communal liv-ing and economic interdependence along with organic gardening and environmentally sustainable projects. While I am pessimistic about a drastic change in global power arrangements in the short term, I am inspired by the many movements that share a progressive global perspective and work tirelessly for justice.

Fourth, I am inspired by the many social movements for a different perspective on the natural environment and human interdependence with animals, plants, and the nonbiological ecosystem of our planet. In response to a growing human perception of environmental crises, young people all over the world have organized themselves into activist groups. A friend who recently completed law school said that the greatest competition among law graduates was for jobs in NGOs that addressed the environment, such as GreenPeace, the Sierra Club, and the National Wildlife Federation.

Most liberal Christians are troubled by the mounting environmental crises such as global warming, pollution of water, air, and land, and unsustainable exploitation of natural resources such as water, wood, oil, coal, and heavy metals. Some progressive Christians joined the "green revolution" of the 1960s and 1970s in support of the use of oil-based fertilizers and genetically modified seeds to grow enough food for the world population. This is a way of accommodating to agribusiness corporations and their understandings of the environment. Other progressive Christians have joined reform movements through the NGOs that are seeking for alternative ways of sustaining the environment through the different use of technology, such as electric cars, wind power, and solar energy. Most Christians have been passive in response to the crises, feeling overwhelmed with the complexity and enormity of the problems, seeing no way to be effective agents, and focusing on their own survival. There are violent responses to the environmental crisis in ecoterrorism, animal rights groups, and individuals such as the Unabomber who sent mail bombs to corporate leaders he perceived as responsible for the ecological disasters. Finally, there are groups who have withdrawn into communities that try to live sustainable and environmentally friendly lives outside of the present corporate structures, not participating in either the productive or consumer economies because of their complicity with environmental disaster. A recent environmental movement is called "Zero Carbon Imprint," in which people try to live off the grid and have no negative effect on the environment. On a less radical level, "The Conservation Fund's Go Zero program offers individuals, corporations and entire communities the tools to measure their carbon dioxide emissions, discover ways to reduce those emissions, and offset the remainder by planting trees."[24] While the range of environmental activist groups contains its own ambiguity, I am inspired by the creative energy and courage that comes from these groups and it gives me courage to face the future.

Fifth, I am inspired by the resistance groups in numerous ethnic and international communities as they assert their cultural identities and global significance as well as their claims for a fair share of economic resources. My own formation as a person and a believer took place in interaction with the African American resistance communities. I was a student in 1965 when the civil rights movement came to Chicago, and I was called to serve a congregation in East Garfield Park, one of the communities where the Southern Christian Leadership Conference was active. At the time, I was searching for a coherent Christian faith that could sustain me in my life of ministry. The sermons during those years brought together Christian evangelical piety with prophetic social justice in a compelling way. I have been a Christian social democrat ever since.

At the same time, the cultural heritage of centuries of resistance against slavery and racism nurtured me. I became a fan of jazz and a student of black intellectual thought. I learned that my white, liberal culture was a social construction with deep contradictions, especially the contradictions of white supremacy and male dominance. In order for my culture to be redeemed from its centuries of domination and exploitation of the resources and peoples of the world, I needed immersion in alternative cultures. Black culture was my first intercultural immersion and it formed me in ways that I still strive to understand. Since then I have immersed myself in women's cultures (the movement to prevent violence against women), Latin American cultures (Nicaragua), and Asian cultures (Korea). These immersion experiences have helped me to relativize my own social location in white, male, liberal, Western, middle-class, Euro-American culture, and to accept accountability for the evil it has perpetuated on the world. I now believe that every human experience is embedded in social and cultural constructions that create the definitions of personal identity and perceptions of the world. In order to understand the mind of Christ, we must immerse ourselves in countercultures and communities of resistance that have nondominant perspectives on the sociopolitical reality of our time.

As a follower of Jesus Christ, I must be able to see my own culture as a partial and ambiguous construction. In addition to cultural difference, there is a history of cultural injustice and cultural domination.[25] For example, American indigenous cultures were deliberately destroyed by the white majority. Indigenous children were taken from their parents and put in missionary schools where they were forbidden to speak their language or practice the rituals of their families of origin. Adult indigenous persons were killed, forced off their land, transported to deserts with lack of resources, and betrayed in thousands of ways.[26] Africans were kidnapped and shipped to the United States where their culture was stolen and their bodies and minds controlled for the sake of their labor. The American indigenous and African American cultures that exist after five hundred years of cultural genocide are resistance cultures. The people live in hybrid situations where traces of their heritage have survived. Sorting out one's identity in these postcolonial situations creates a vigorous debate within the resistance communities about what is authentic and hope filled.[27] I have learned from my own immersion experiences that my white Euro-American culture is likewise hybrid with traces of integrity mixed in with layer after layer of distortions and contradictions. For me, understanding God as relational, ambiguous, and resilient helps me survive in this cultural matrix.

> What social movements give you hope for a better history for your own country and the global community of nations?

I have outlined some social movements that give me hope because they have developed a hopeful perspective on the current sociopolitical situation. Christians are often active in these groups because of their discipleship to Jesus Christ. What counts as hopeful in any particular historical epoch depends on one's vision of how God works with humans in the world, and depends on how a community assesses its social location in relation to power and oppression.

To be confessional, I sometimes have found myself in each of the five strategies of hope in community and global crisis. But increasingly I have moved away from accommodation and withdrawal as I have watched the multiple crises of our time develop. Too often I find myself in the survival camp because I have been personally rewarded with tenure, salary, health benefits, and pension as I have taught and published my ideas. In my inner spirit, however, I vacillate between the reform camp and the revolt camp. I read the news and journals for signs of reform that might avert the disasters and lead to more justice in the world. I fervently pray that radical reforms or revolution will come to pass. In my most pessimistic moments, I become apocalyptic and believe that the world as we know it will bring Armageddon and hope will be reborn from local initiatives. Finding hope during a time of global crisis is not an easy endeavor.

In faith I believe God is bringing a new future that will transform the reality we know and assume to be permanent. In order to perceive this future, we must live in faith and trust in God. This means abandoning our faith in the promises of empires and established leaders and instead trusting in the movement of God's Holy Spirit in new ways. God is preserving the past so that what is good will never be lost. God is creating a novel future that has possibilities we cannot imagine. In faith, we can live with a vision of hope that does not deny the danger of our present situation.

For Christians, "Christ grounds the hope that what we now experience is not the final possibility for humanity."[28] I believe that though I cannot see a future arising out of the present, God in Christ has already sent new forms of embodiment that are transformative in creation. "Faithfulness to Christ requires immersion in the secular and pluralistic consciousness . . . and it is precisely here that Christ now works, impeded by our failure to recognize him and by our continuing association of faith with past, particularized expressions of Christ."[29] Even when my own hope fails to sustain me, I have hope because God in Christ gives me hope that goes beyond everything I can see and imagine. I see the signs already. Praise be to God!

SUMMARY

In this chapter, I have confessed my own struggle with eschatology, the presence of hope in the future. My process theology requires me to look for hope in the empirical world in which I live, not just in fantasies about how God will rescue me from history. So I must examine the historical moments in which I live and find signs that God's love and power are bringing about a new future of which I can be a part. The twenty-first century is a challenging time to be a Christian believer because of socio-political violence of our age. Looking for hope requires deep honesty as we confess our social location in the real world. In the next chapter, I look at the smaller communities of local congregations for signs of faithful practice and hopeful faith. Most Christians practice their faith in congregations, and here we find everyday faithfulness.

SEVEN
Congregational
Practices of Hope

Practical theology begins with a study of Christian practices. In this project, I have looked specifically at the stories of Linda, Philip, and other survivors of family violence, and shared some of my own religious experiences. I have developed constructive theologies about God, sin and evil, Jesus Christ, Holy Spirit, church, and eschatology. In each of these discussions I have used three authorities: Scripture, systematic theology, and contemporary practices of faith. Now I will make suggestions about what difference these ideas make in local congregations. Practical theology begins with practice and ends with practice. In between practical theologians engage with multiple conversation partners including philosophers, theologians, psychologists, and others.

As Christian communities, how do we connect the social movements of hope to practices of hope in our daily lives? Below I examine four areas of congregational practice: arts and worship, Christian education, pastoral care, and prophetic signs and social action. What would it mean to engage in practices that are consistent with the five marks of the church discussed in chapter 6: inclusive love, empowering justice, nonviolent resistant to evil, multiplicity and unity, ambiguity and goodness?

ARTS AND WORSHIP

In the arts and worship, I often find signs of human resistance to evil and visions of a world of nonviolence and justice. In my lifetime, I have seen dramatic changes in prayers, sermons, hymns, and many rituals of the church. One of the most dramatic has been the use of inclusive language for God and humans. I believe that changing the language about gender will reduce the violence against women, especially when combined with long-term social movements for gender justice. The New Revised Standard Version of the Bible uses inclusive language for human beings, though it tends to preserve male language for God. Likewise, there has been a dramatic increase in awareness of race and culture in our liturgies. Offensive images such as use of the word *white* to mean good, and the use of the word *black* to mean bad have been avoided in many churches. There is a general awareness that racial and cultural prejudices and discrimination have existed in the church, and that our prayers and hymns should reflect the multiplicity of Christians in the world without the bias of one superior culture.

Much work needs to be done. Feminist scholars from many countries have shown that some theological images continue to perpetuate prejudice based on gender, race, and culture. For example, the church is very fond of employing the image of servanthood to convey that church leaders should respond to the needs of the people, not consider their office as a status symbol, and not use their power for control over others. However, there is less attention to the issue of economic servanthood in the world of work. In our time, female immigrants from Latin America and Asia are much more likely to be employed as servants in homes, hospitals, and restaurants without significant power to determine their schedules, pay, health care, and family needs. Servanthood has potential to become a spiritualized concept that does not deal with discrimination based on gender, race, class, and culture. When we call Christians to become servants, we usually do not mean that they should enter the servant class and work for low-wage jobs without social power. In fact, we use the word *servant* to refer to persons with high status, which can result in hiding their real power inequities in the community.[1] There are similar discussions among feminist theologians about concepts such as sacrifice, suffering, obedience, and images of family that promise ongoing theological reform.

One of the most difficult issues for worship has been language about God. Many theologians agree that male language for God is metaphorical,

What practices of worship give you courage and hope in the midst of personal and social challenges?

using familiar human images to point to characteristics of God. As the creator of the world, God is beyond gender. God cannot be defined by gender, and there is gender equality in the kin-dom of God. Therefore, it makes sense to me that we critically evaluate our references to God as Father because this metaphor does not exhaust what it means to say that God is Creator and shares the intimacy of a parent with human beings. It is surely an accident of history that many languages of the world are organized by gender so that even hammers and nails have gender in some languages. Even if *Abba* or Father was a favorite image of God for Jesus, he was working within the limitations of language and culture of the time. Beyond that, the gender of Jesus was accidental and should not be seen as essential to his role as the second member of the Trinity who brought salvation to the world. Surely, the Trinity is beyond gender. Yet, many churches in the world today argue that women cannot be ordained ministers in the church because Jesus was male, and only a male can fully represent God. As long as the church discriminates against female human beings in language and leadership, the larger society will discriminate against women as a social class and violence against women will remain endemic. We can begin a move toward gender justice by using inclusive images of God, Jesus, and the Holy Spirit.[2]

To illustrate this point, I include here a revision of the Lord's Prayer as developed through the communal process of a local congregation in Evanston, Illinois. They worked together to revise their weekly ritual prayer to correspond to some of the values they hold most dearly as Christians.[3]

> O God
> Who is within us and beyond us,
> Holy are your names
> Your new earth come
> Your will be done
> On earth as it is in promise.
> Give us this day our daily bread
> And forgive us our Sin
> As we forgive those who sin against us.
> Help us to resist temptation
> And deliver us from evil
> For yours is the New Earth
> And the power and the glory forever. Amen.

CHRISTIAN EDUCATION

Second, local congregations have responsibility for educating children
and adults in the Christian faith. The practical theological discipline of
Christian education has worked diligently for many decades to evaluate critically the powerful social sciences that have developed in the last
150 years. Modern psychology has transformed contemporary society,
changing the ways we view child and adult development, sexuality, moral
development, and faith development. We understand much better how
children are formed by society, and how adults are shaped by gender,
race, class, and culture. We also know, however, that the normative ideas
of the social sciences are embedded in the assumptions of Enlightenment
ideas that favor individualism, materialism, and secularism. Whether the
social sciences are compatible with Christian faith is highly contested
within the United States. And when U.S. Christians encounter other cultures formed with alternative assumptions, major debates occur.

For example, there is a huge debate about children and parenting between conservative Christians such as James Dobson, founder of
Focus on the Family,[4] and mainline Christian denominations such as
Presbyterians and Methodists. Focus on the Family believes that children are vulnerable to temptations from the devil because of original
sin. That is, children are likely to make unhealthy and immoral choices
if they are allowed to exercise their free will without restraint. Therefore, Focus on the Family recommends "tough love" that provides clear
moral teaching for children and punishes them for wrong choices. Parents need to be clear role models, demonstrating moral righteousness
and providing punishments (harsh, if necessary) for children who do
not respect moral authority.

In contrast, Christian educators in mainline denominations tend
to believe that children can be trusted to make good judgments if they
are given a positive environment of love and encouragement.[5] Within
relationships that embody basic respect for their dignity, children will
often make good choices, and when they don't they should be corrected
with loving consequences they can understand at their level of cognitive development. These educators believe that children are more likely
to stray from righteousness when they experience rejection and abuse
of adult power. These two approaches to education of children have
different theological assumptions that go back beyond modern social

sciences. For example, in the mid-nineteenth century, Horace Bushnell[8] advocated permissive styles of parenting that were controversial at the time because he challenged the Calvinistic emphasis on original sin.

Based on the five marks of the church, I take sides with those from the mainline denominations and a more permissive psychology of child education. When Jesus interacted with children, he showed compassion and support, not judgment and punishment. Ched Myers says that Jesus promoted an ethic of nonviolence in the family through his teachings on children and his attitudes on marriage, sexuality, and anger. The mark of multiplicity means that parents and teachers dare not understand children as possessions they can shape to their own purposes. Rather, children are others, full human beings with their own mystery, who have been created in the image of God and created for their own purposes in the world. Parents are called to love their children, but are admonished not to use them for their own narcissistic needs. The value of ambiguity means that all parenting is confusing and difficult, and parents should be humble about their ability to understand their children. Children grow up with their own perceptions of themselves, others, and the society in which they live. They receive their own call from God that the parents may not be able to understand. Therefore, parents must respect their children as other than themselves, and as ambiguous in their morality from the parent's perspective. Parents must use nonviolence in their parenting without assuming that they know what God is doing in a child's life.

> What practices of Christian education have you found empowering in your local congregation?

What would it mean to include all children as full members of a congregation, to treat all children with justice and nonviolence, to respect their otherness and ambiguity? Fortunately, the discipline of Christian education provides many resources that are consistent with these values.

PASTORAL CARE

Third, pastoral care is a central mission of local congregations. The local congregation is called to be a caring and healing community, a place where its members feel safe, where the best ideals of family life are enacted, and where strangers and aliens can receive hospitality. Most churches engage in significant ministries of pastoral care—visiting the sick, comforting the dying and bereaved, advising families, parents, youth and young children, and helping marriages through challenging transitions. The discipline of pastoral care has produced guidebooks on almost every topic that Christians face as they struggle to be faithful. An example of the contribution of pastoral care is the progress we have made on understanding and preventing sexual and domestic violence.

I have worked in the United States and in multiple cultures in Latin America and Asia to develop models of pastoral care for families experiencing domestic violence. I have worked closely with the Faith Trust Institute, an ecumenical, interreligious agency that focuses on the religious issues of sexual and domestic violence.[7] In addition, I am a member of the Black Mountain Presbyterian Church, which has developed its own policy regarding domestic violence ministries, including an active committee to educate the congregation and the local community on the prevention of domestic violence.[8] Here are excerpts from the local church statement, passed in 2001 by this congregation's Session:

> In obedience to Christ's call for Black Mountain Presbyterian Church to respond to abuse as a matter of justice and righteousness, we will hear the voices of victims and survivors and respond to their calls with the following goals: first, to work to protect victims from further abuse; second, to stop the abuser's violence and hold the abuser accountable; and third, to restore the family relationship if possible or mourn the loss of relationship.

The statement goes on to develop specific strategies and programs for implementation in the congregation. Some of these strategies include:

- to provide adequate training for pastors, church officers, caregivers, and volunteers to recognize and respond appropriately to domestic violence.

- to educate children, youth, and adult members about the availability of local domestic violence resources, and to communicate that specific trained church personnel are available to discuss past, existing, or potential domestic violence.

- to regularly preach about domestic violence through the ministry of the pulpit.

- to address domestic violence often and regularly through liturgy, prayers, stories, testimonies, minutes for mission, information printed in newsletters and the guide to worship; thematic workshops, Bible studies, and Sunday school presentations.

After these commitments, the statement becomes very specific: "two worship services (per year) addressing domestic violence and the response of the faith community; a mailing to all members stating the position of the church, with open letters to victims, perpetrators, and children; consider adding an outreach ministry to families in Black Mountain who are facing domestic violence."

This is one example of what a local congregation can do to address actively an issue of violence in the local community in a way that affects the lives of real people. By addressing both the pastoral care and social justice sides of family life, the congregation becomes more aware of how every family is called to be nonviolent, and how the church is called to be more aware of how abuse of power affects people according to gender, race, class, and disabilities. Understanding pastoral care as a social justice issue can transform all aspects of a congregation's program.

A difficult issue for some local congregations is how to provide pastoral care and accountability for persons who are known to be sex offenders—for example, persons who have served prison terms for sexual crimes. There are many sex offenders who are not known to the congregation or the criminal justice system. The following is a statement adopted by a U.S. congregation that tried to respond to the issue of how to provide support and accountability for members who were known sex offenders.

Behavioral Covenant [with a sex offender] for the XYW Church

Seeking to be faithful in community with one another, this covenant will help us to be attentive to the guidelines and conditions necessary to provide a safe environment in which all can feel the welcome of Jesus Christ.

I agree to attend the Traditional Sunday Worship Service (11:00 A.M.) accompanied by a court/church-approved Supervisor.

I agree to meet my Supervisor promptly in front of my house at 10:45 A.M. on Sunday mornings. The Supervisor will pull up in front of my home and use the car horn to announce his/her arrival. I understand that they will wait a maximum of 5 minutes. If I am unable to meet the time schedule on a given morning, I will not be able to attend church that morning.

I agree NOT to personally contact the Supervisors or members of the Supervisory Committee. A Supervisor or staff member will contact me with any pertinent information concerning a change in the schedule or program.

I agree to comply with all conditions set forth by the Office of Probation and Parole and the conditions of the XYZ congregation:

- I understand that *No Contact* with children includes verbal, emotional, and physical contact, and mental grooming.

- I understand that a child is anyone under the age of 18 years.

- I will attend the 11:00 A.M. Worship Service in the Sanctuary.

- I will attend Sunday Worship accompanied by court/church-approved supervisors.

- I will not be on church property at any other time.

- I will remain within 5 feet of my Supervisor at all times while in the church facility.

- I will only use the private bathroom on the main (Sanctuary) level of the church.

- I will sit in the balcony of the Sanctuary, organ side, closest to the window wall.

- If I want to attend a special service held at a time other than 11:00 A.M. on a Sunday morning, that request can be made to the Supervisor who in turn, will alert a member of the Supervisory Committee. This decision would be made by the committee in consultation with Session.

- I understand that all conditions and guidelines remain the same for special services.

- I will be part of a Small Group. The group will be a community of personal, spiritual support offering study and Christian fellowship.

- I agree to honor and abide by this covenant.

- I acknowledge my responsibility to be a faithful participant in this program.

Signature _____

Witnesses: _____ [9]

Such statements about sex offenders have been received with mixed results: some survivors of violence fear that such policies are too lenient and do not protect children who might accidentally meet perpetrators at a local shopping mall and consider them a safe person because of their connection to the church. Some survivors are not comfortable worshiping with someone who reminds them of the acute pain from their own childhood. Some church members feel that all sex offenders should be in prison and not allowed to jeopardize the safety of innocent people. On the other hand, some abusers reject the guidance described here because they feel it dehumanizes them and the statement is naïve about the presence of other sex offenders who have not been exposed for public scrutiny. These abusers assert the right to some anonymity so they can begin to organize a more normal life, find adequate employment, and have similar personal freedoms as other adults in the community. Many churches are in the midst of a debate about the correct way Christian groups should respond to the reality of sexual and domestic violence. How this gets resolved is a matter of practice over time within the Christian community.

The Mennonite chaplains in the Canadian national prison system have developed a church-based program for sex offenders called *Circles of Support and Accountability.* It involves developing a covenant between sex offenders soon to be released from jail and providing support for obtaining housing, jobs, and networks of relationships that can facilitate a transition to life after prison. They also include clear forms of accountability to provide safety for the community. The training and guidelines for this program are a model for other groups interested in safety and compassion for survivors and offenders.[10]

What prophetic pastoral care practices in local congregations have you seen?

PROPHETIC SIGNS AND SOCIAL ACTION

A fourth way that congregations can embody the marks of the church include organizing prophetic signs and social programs for the salvation of the whole world. As a congregation becomes more aware of issues of inclusive love, empowering justice, nonviolent resistance to evil, multiplicity and unity, and ambiguity and goodness in its internal and family relationships, it begins to connect with the larger social justice issues in the local community. The principle of inclusive love means that local congregations listen carefully to their members and neighbors about the social context in which they live. Individuals and families frequently face gender discrimination, racial prejudice, and class oppression. These struggles often require pastoral care and educational responses. Congregations should be alert to the need for prophetic action. In fact, many congregations have standing committees that work on larger social issues that affect the quality of daily life in local communities.

First Presbyterian Church in Evanston, Illinois, has an environment committee with two goals: (a) to improve the environmental practices of families and the church building itself; and (b) to monitor local, regional, national, and global issues that need responses from the church members. Below is the description of their program:

Environmental Stewardship

Mission Statement

The Environmental Stewardship Work Group provides resources for the First Presbyterian Church of Evanston's ecological directives. We pledge to take action in keeping with Biblical teachings on Creation Care in order to increase our understanding, celebration, and stewardship of God's good earth in home, congregation, community, and state.

> *"For since the creation of the world God's invisible qualities—his eternal power and divine nature—have been clearly seen, being understood from what has been made, so that men are without excuse." Romans 1:20*

Get Involved

Yes, we recycle old church bulletins, printer cartridges, and cell phones! Contact _____ for details.

Did You Know?

Our Fellowship Hour at church is now more just and sustainable? The Deacons have switched from styrofoam cups to compostable cups, also our coffee is now purchased from Cafe Justos, a mission that encourages Mexican farmers to stay on their ancestral lands by providing a fair wage for their products.

We also invite you to calculate your family's environmental impact and then find creative ways to be a more responsible steward of God's creation.

Find Out More

We welcome new participants to our group. The only requirement is a sincere interest in environmental and conservation issues. All members ages 15 and up are welcome; senior high and college students are encouraged to get involved. You can also find out more by contacting the church office.[11]

The Evanston church partners with the city to help families think about how they can achieve a "zero footprint" on the environment. The city's Web page includes a one-minute calculator for a family's carbon footprint and provides Internet links to partners who deal with the environment.

Lutheran School of Theology in Chicago (LSTC), through their "Green Seminary Project," is one of the national leaders in the church's environmental movement. By engaging seminary students during their formative education, LSTC hopes to influence a generation of local congregational leaders to understand the theological importance of the environment for the future. LSTC has had a major impact on other seminaries and denominations.[12]

Environmental action is one prophetic action local congregations can take to educate their members and engage in prophet social action. There are many other issues that capture the attention of members of local congregations. For example, the same Evanston congregation has many mission groups focusing on a variety of prophetic social issues, including mission prayer, the Muslim world, Bethlehem Sister Church, prison ministries, China, the Congo, International Friends student ministry, environmental stewardship, Middle East Fellowship, a warming center, and urban missions. This list shows what one congregation is doing to educate its members in discipleship and engage them in prophetic social action. Such programs are multiplied by thousands of congregations throughout the world.

Another example is Trinity United Church of Christ in Chicago, which has organized itself as a "full-service church" in response to the needs of the local African American community and the spiritual and economic needs of African Americans in the world. Below is a partial list of the multiple ministries aimed at educating their members and engaging them in active ministries to improve the local community and the health of the larger African diaspora.[13]

Ministries Created to Assist in the Transformation of Our Community

1. Active Seniors: programs for seniors in the community
2. Adopt-a-Student: care of college students
3. Athletes for Christians: local sports activities for health
4. Career Development: job counseling and training
5. Church in Society: prophetic political activism
6. Domestic Violence, Advocacy/Care: referral, emergency shelter, counseling, training
7. Drug and Alcohol Recovery: referral, counseling, 12-step groups
8. Food Share: food supplies distributed through the local church
9. Grandparent's Ministry
10. HIV/AIDS Support: support, education, training
11. Housing: seminars to support home ownership and solve housing problems
12. Immabasi (Health and Well-being): educating professions and congregations on community health issues.
13. Micah Legal Ministry: advance human and civil rights through education and activism
14. Math Tutorial: education program for vulnerable children.
15. Men Allied in Christ
16. Million for the Master: partnering with groups in the community for economic development.
17. Prison Ministry: visiting prisons, corresponding with prisoners, helping families with members in prison, helping prisoners after release.
18. Project Jeremiah: Mentoring program for youth
19. Reading Tutorial: education program for vulnerable children.
20. Village Keepers

African Culture Ministries

1. Africa

2. Caribbean

3. Chinara

4. Drama

5. Fine Arts and Literature

6. Intonjane: rites of passage program for young women

7. Isuthu: rites of passage program for young men

8. Tangeni Adult Dance: African dance for worship and performance

9. Walaika: Children's Choir

First Presbyterian Church and Trinity United Church of Christ are two local congregations who call their members to actively practice inclusive love, empowering justice, nonviolent resistance to evil, multiplicity and unity, ambiguity and goodness. They themselves are ambiguous institutions with their own contradictions. The programs they have instituted are criticized and contested in many ways by those who have other visions. I submit that there is no way to be an activist follower of Jesus without causing controversy and embodying many contradictions that must be continually faced honestly.

> How does your local congregation help you witness to Jesus Christ on contemporary social problems?

SUMMARY

In this chapter I have focused on congregational practices of hope. In spite of the many challenges in the world that arise from evil systems of gender, race, class, culture, and environmental degradation, congregations have organized themselves with energetic and creative responses. In the academy, disciplines of Christian education, arts and worship, pastoral care, and prophetic social action have encouraged activism on behalf of persons that experience oppression and suffering in the world. Congregations have developed many forms of faithful practice in order to express the relational, ambiguous, and resilient love and power of God in Jesus Christ.

Conclusion
The Beauty of God

I recently read a story by a woman who lost her faith in God after her younger brother died as a young adult. She could not reconcile this tragic loss with her image of God as all-powerful and all-knowing. She went for several years in a confused religious state, worrying about how she would pull through. In a class on creating a sustainable environment from the perspective of process theology, she returned to her love for God. In order to express the faith she learned from years of grief and loss, she developed a cognitive view of God as relational, ambiguous, and resilient who could understand the painful suffering of her life, and from that she developed a spirituality that was healing. In her own words:

> Once I had found an idea of God that made sense to me . . . the next step
> was to find a spirituality that called to me. . . . I now have a definition of
> spirituality: a pure connection to self, nature, or other humans that stems from
> compassion. By working this out, I was able to once again feel my spiritual self
> stirring inside me; it was as if by defining spirituality, I woke up the need to feel
> it once again. Once the need was awake, it was able to begin to be fulfilled.[1]

The basic theological reform I am calling for is that we understand God as a partner in the ongoing process of a living creation. God is real, and therefore God is a part of the relational, ambiguous process that characterizes our lives. God is not subject to all the same limitations we face in human life because God is an ongoing part of the creativity itself and we are only moments within the process. But God is *relational*—that is, God is embedded within the relationality of everything that exists. God is *ambiguous*—that is, God cannot know the full reality of the future and accepts accountability for the consequences of multiple free decisions. God is *resilient*—that is, God survives forever, and through God's resilience, we have hope for love and power in a future we cannot control. Whatever tragedy emerges in history, God is not destroyed, and God's love creates new moments of contrast and harmony that lead to beauty. Because of God's love and power, the world of beauty is constantly recreated, and we are called to enjoy and worship signs of the beauty of the world as it is, even as we strive for healing and value that transcends our present reality.

THE BEAUTY OF THE MULTIPLE GOD

Since retirement in 2008, I have become interested in bird watching. It gives me a chance to slow down, get out in nature, and focus on something completely new to exercise my brain. I have learned that birders have seen 469 bird species of birds in North Carolina and the list keeps expanding.[2] Worldwide, there are ten thousand species of birds. I assume the lists of other animals and plants in the world is likewise diverse. As I watch birds, I notice most of all their beauty—the various colors, shapes, markings, behaviors, and songs that distinguish them from all other birds. Scientists are constantly discovering and reevaluating the categories of birds because they discover new ways birds are related to one another and new ways they are different.

Why does God want so many birds? My theological answer is that God loves multiplicity. Whitehead is correct: the direction of creativity is toward more complexity—"the many become one and are increased by one." The increase by one is always distinctive because no other moment has exactly the same internal structure and context as any other moment. Birds are constantly coming into being and dying off, and always moving toward a multiplicity of forms. Environmental pollution is evil because it threatens God's love of multiplicity. Some species become extinct because of the finitude built into creation; but some species become extinct because of human abuse of power, thus creating genuine tragedy. Evil is the destruction of bodies and spirits, whether mineral, plant, or animal. In this sense, evil events are enemies of God because they work against the creative love of God toward multiplicity.

By analogy, human beings with their diverse cultures, languages, religions, and desires show God's love of multiplicity. Until the middle of the twentieth century, Western culture seemed to despise multiplicity and was driven toward an imaginary universal homogeneity. Nineteenth-century Christian missionaries were motivated to "spread the gospel" and "evangelize the world" and they were not sufficiently open to the differences of local cultures and religions. Likewise, Western corporations and governments want to control earth's resources for their own benefit regardless of effects on local people and their ways of life.

The name for this Western drive for homogenization is *colonialism*. At the time when colonialism was official public policy, it was understood to mean bringing the advantages of Western culture and technology to uncivilized peoples in the world. Later, critics challenged colonialism because it almost always meant exploiting local resources for the benefit of global empires and the transfer of wealth from poor to wealthy nations and corporations. However, local people never give up their wish to preserve their particularity.

Today we use the term *postcolonialism* to designate the end of the era of domination, and also to refer to the ambiguous effects of the long period of colonial domination. If modernity refers to the Western belief in unity and universality, then postmodernity refers to the love of multiplicity and particularity. Obviously, we live in a time when cultural domination remains strong and local cultures struggle for survival. If God loves multiplicity, then the church should ally itself with love of particularity and oppose the drive toward a universal homogeneity that destroys local cultures and communities. I can worship a God who loves multiplicity because I also love multiplicity and the challenge of finding harmony and unity in the midst of diversity.

> Do you think God loves multiplicity? What difference does it make?

THE BEAUTY OF THE AMBIGUOUS GOD

Because God has real relationships and loves multiplicity, the actual world is ambiguous. That is, multiple centers of freedom create conflicting centers of value, and individual decisions actually influence the future, creating consequences that have conflicting values that potentially violate the creativity of future moments. Since God is an actor in the process of becoming, God shares moral responsibility for the consequences of history. In this sense, God is an ambiguous figure as perceived by humans and as an actor in history. Loomer is correct to say that a concrete God who is ambiguous is more real than an abstract God who is perfect. To that I would add, a concrete God who is ambiguous is beautiful.

I have learned about the beauty of the ambiguous God from survivors of violence. Linda grew up in a family that tried to destroy her body and spirit. Before Linda developed any self-awareness, her mother took pleasure in causing her physical pain and blamed her for resisting. Like many abusers, Linda's mother wanted her daughter's compliance with her own destruction in order to rationalize the violence she imposed on her. Linda learned to be passive and cooperative during episodes of physical and sexual abuse in order to minimize the pain she would suffer. In this sense, her silence and passivity was a form of resistance for survival. Even though she was unable to prevent the violence, she withheld her will privately. However, Linda was betrayed by her own body and she learned to associate sexual pleasure with torture. Later, when she was a teenager, she was revictimized by sexual abuse from adult men in the community and she used drugs to numb the physical and emotional pain she felt. She suffered daily, but miraculously survived. From such a childhood, Linda knows the meaning of ambiguity. She inherited conflicting values from her experience that continue to shape her physical and spiritual life. She struggles to resist the inner pull of her mother's influence as she dedicates her life to doing good in the midst of ambiguity. She uses her deep knowledge of ambiguity and goodness to help other survivors and to help congregations become communities of love and care.

Philip learned ambiguity in a different way. He grew up in a small town in Alabama in a poor African American community. His mother was a single parent who died when he was nine years old and he was raised by his grandmother and aunt. The family and a racist society created many obstacles for Philip's education and development. His emotional life was neglected and he witnessed constant violence and emotional abuse between his grandmother and aunt. He went to church and school during the tense years of southern adjustment to the new civil rights laws. As a sensitive, gay young male, Philip felt a calling to education and leadership, but his chronic depression prevented him from reaching his goals. As a young adult, Philip was strongly influenced by mentors who were sexually abusive toward younger African American males. When he followed their lead and acted abusively toward students in his care, he was arrested, imprisoned, and stigmatized as a sex offender. He suffered through eight years of harsh imprisonment without appropriate treatment or education and four years of probation. Today he struggles to find employment and housing for minimal survival. He also struggles to find friends he can trust and a church where he feels comfortable. It is very difficult for Philip as a gay African American male who has been stigmatized as a sex offender. Philip's life is full of internal and external ambiguity. Philip has amazing insights into the ambiguity of human life, but he is prevented from using his wisdom to help others. His innate abilities and rich experiences may never be accepted by a society looking for easy answers to the complex problem of sexual violence.

Linda and Philip and many other survivors help me to understand that every human being is caught in the middle of ambiguity. Like them, I have inherited ambiguous desires and values from my family of origin, and I have made mistakes as a husband, parent, pastor, and teacher because of what I inherited and the decisions I made about how to understand myself and the world. Like Linda and Philip, I inherited an ambiguous historical situation as a white male in a patriarchal U.S. culture wedded to white supremacy and global domination. My privilege is the result of decades of violence toward women and people of color, and in many ways I have participated in perpetuating the system because of its benefits for me. Both the inheritance from the past and my own decisions about the future have been ambiguous. My health and goodness depend on my ability to perceive, evaluate, and respond creatively to what I have received. Facing ambiguity is one of the hardest things I have ever done. Accepting the ambiguity I have received and the ambiguity I have passed on requires courage. This is why ambiguity has become such an important value for me. I can only engage in good choices when I am able to face the ambiguity I have received and that I perpetuate on others. I must be accountable for what I receive and what I pass on in order to see myself and the world as it really is.

I believe that God faces a similar ambiguity. Because God is real, God inherits ambiguity from many free decisions made by individuals.

There is no time or place where everything is ideal and perfect; things are always a confusing muddle of contradictory values and desires. God is faced with choosing how to act in the midst of a muddle. In theory there are always better and worse ways of responding to the ambiguity of the past, but no guarantee that everything will be good because multiple decisions influence the future. What God intends for good can be used for evil by human beings. What human beings intend for evil is often turned into good by God (Gen. 50:20). Just as God does not control the actual past because of the multiple decision makers, so God does not control the future because the future depends on how multiple decisions are made in the future. In the moment of making a decision, an individual can act with courage and righteousness, but individuals often act with indifference and intent of evil and violence toward others and the web of life. God is caught in a world of relative values and the choices God makes help to determine the future, which is always ambiguous.

Can I worship a God who is subject to ambiguity? Yes, I can. In fact, it gives me hope to believe that God cares deeply about the actual world and that God is involved in trying to create a better world in the midst of tragedy and evil. I can believe that God shared the pain that Linda experienced as a child and accompanied her through the long years of abuse and violence she experienced. I can believe that God knows the internal and external oppression of Philip's life and helped him survive so far. I can believe that God understood the painful struggles I have had in my life. God calls all of us to greater awareness and courage because God suffers with us but without despair. God is not defeated by ambiguity in the same way that threatens us. God knows that the spirit of life endures and will endure to struggle another day, even when there is genuine tragedy.

Ambiguity is clearly a part of human life. Can ambiguity really apply to God?

There is no way to bring back the twelve million people who died in Nazi concentration camps, but the ones who survived the war did not forget what happened and they helped to create a new world. Genocide has not been eliminated from human history, but many testify to its evil reality and work to bring about a different future than Hitler wanted. God accepts ambiguity as the reality of the actual world, both in the past and the future, but never gives up striving for good.

THE BEAUTY OF THE RESILIENT GOD

I believe in a God of love and power who never gives up. In the actual world, individual moments have freedom to influence the future. This creates the potential for incredible diversity and beauty, and it also creates the potential for tragedy and evil. In a world where we all influence one another for good or evil, it is a beautiful thing when a diverse community of individuals creates harmony between the many contrasts and contradictions. In a world where the human spirit shapes the real world, those who survive evil and live to create another day can help to harmonize the contradictions. Theologian Bernard Loomer said that Jesus can be our model of full humanity because he was able to harmonize the contradictions of love and hate, life and death, without being destroyed.[3] The resurrection is God's affirmation of the value of Jesus' life and death. Jesus achieved great beauty in the midst of great evil and thus serves as a model for what is possible in human life. The stories saved by the church inspire new generations to understand the resilience of God regardless of the circumstances.

I believe in the resilience of God because of the witness of communities of resistance. Individual survivors I have known should not have survived, and they speak on behalf of many others who did not survive—children were killed, adult survivors committed suicide, died from substance abuse, or developed mental disorders that made them repeated victims and abusers. The survivors show that systematic abuse of a whole class of people (including women, African Americans, Indigenous peoples) does not destroy the love and power of God. For those who live and seek life, God responds with creative possibilities for healing. Many women and men have survived abuse and become creative leaders of society. As we develop a public forum on abuse, more and more leaders will be free to speak about their encounters with abuse and how they were able to overcome evil imposed on their lives.

My study of the Holocaust promulgated by Nazi Germany helps me to understand the resilient power and love of God. From the survivors of this horror has come amazing leadership in society, religion, arts, and literature about the nature of human life. How is it possible for such creativity and beauty to rise from such evil? To me, it means that there is something in the human spirit that is resilient. There is something good in human beings that cannot be totally overcome. We are indebted to those who saw death on a scale new in human history and lived to create new life for themselves and others. For me, this is witness to the resilience of the power and love of God. Because God shares power with human beings and the creation itself, the evil of the Holocaust could not be prevented. Many people ignored the dangers and colluded with the Nazis as they organized the Holocaust. God absorbed the suffering of the world war and created possibilities for those who survived.

I am deeply influenced by the narrative of the African American community since 1492 when Columbus brought the first African slaves to the new world. For 350 years the United States and other governments organized and defended slavery. The United States invented a new system of human oppression based on color from which neither adults nor children born into slavery could ever hope to gain freedom. Individual owners had the power of life and death over human beings, and the Africans enslaved in this system had no legal right to complain or present their grievances. In the 1850s the Supreme Court, in the Dred Scott case, required even the northern states where slavery was illegal to hunt down human beings who escaped from slavery and return them to their masters. The daily reality of slavery included rape, mutilation, physical punishment, and denial of food, medical care, education, and religious freedom. It was one of the most evil systems of human control and abuse ever devised and it lasted for seventeen generations. After the Civil War that killed 600,000 to 700,000 human beings and disabled thousands more, African Americans, who became U.S. Citizens in 1866, were forced into a system of apartheid and segregation characterized by violence, threats, and severe discrimination.

In your experience, what are the empirical signs that God is resilient?

Even today, over forty years after the civil rights legislation of 1968 that ended apartheid in the United States, many African Americans live in conditions of poverty that continue the legacy of slavery.

The resilience of the African American community has been inspiring for me. Out of the evil of the slave system has come the most beautiful art, music, literature, dance, and creative social projects. In spite of historical efforts of the white society to destroy everything African

in the United States including its people, the creativity of the African
American community has become decisive for U.S. culture and politics.
What was denied has become integral to the identity of U.S. communal
personality and influence in the world.

The fact that nonviolent resistance to evil was at the center of the
African American community and its witness is especially inspiring for
me. The ability to endure a great suffering imposed by evil forces, to
endure over generations, and to offer the community gifts for others is
instructive of my doctrine of God. I see the same resilient love and power
in the life of Jesus, to which the African American Christian churches
point as the source of their inspiration. Of course, the African American
community is filled with multiplicity and ambiguity and resilience. There
is probably no community I know of that is more aware of the diversity
of individuals and identities, and that accepts ambiguity as a part of life.

Harriett Jacobs's autobiography of life during slavery and after
escaping features ambiguity at its core.[4] In order to survive slavery, Ms.
Jacobs had to violate her own moral code and, regardless of her courageous actions, she could not prevent her children from becoming slaves.
Her story discloses the evil system she lived under—evil was embedded
in her family, her master's family, the local churches, the African American community, the town of Edenton, the state of North Carolina, and
the national government. The white lover she took to protect her from
the violence of her master became a U.S. congressman of high status, yet
he did nothing to support her in freedom or to provide for her children
before and after the Civil War. Yet she survived and became a national
leader in educating children after the end of slavery. Her life bore the
scars of the evil she experienced, but her courage has been inspiring for
many generations. Just as the evil of slavery cannot be explained since
it goes against every value that sustains human life, so the resilience of
people like Harriett Jacobs cannot be explained because, as poet Audre
Lorde wrote, she "was not meant to survive."[5]

Because of Harriett Jacobs and the millions of other survivors of
evil, I believe in the resilient, ambiguous God who was revealed in Jesus
Christ and who lives through human beings whenever evil is resisted
and goodness is embodied. This is the God I worship and adore. I pray
that the Holy Spirit will occasionally be evident in my own life and decisions for the glory of God.

Methods of Practical Theology
for Congregations and Church Leaders

Every Christian who seriously tries to practice her or his faith is doing practical theology. Being a Christian means trying to live one's life according to one's best understanding of what the Bible teaches about what God wants us to do and find appropriate ways to live this faith in the world. We try to match our everyday lives with what God wants.

Teachers are called by the church to train church leaders for their tasks as practical theologians. Scholars are called by the church with responsibility for research on the issues facing the church and development of practical theology as an academic theological discipline.

In the appendices that follow, I define the steps involved in practical theological thinking at congregational and professional levels.[1] In

> What are the appropriate methods for engaging in practical theology in local congregations? How are these methods shaped by the Scriptures and traditions of the church and the situation in which we find ourselves in the world?

this appendix I discuss two levels of method: level-one method for local congregations, and level-two method for church leaders in local churches and judicatories. In the following appendix I discuss level-three method for teachers and scholars in practical theology.

Living faithful Christian lives is not a simple matter because we are faced with decisions about confusing situations and we must cooperate with other people when we don't understand either ourselves or the others. It is not an easy matter to understand our own motives for what we do, to have valid insights into the motives of others, and to know what to do when we are faced with contradictory information and painful consequences. It has long been part of Christian wisdom that we need to be active members of local communities of faith so that we can be in constant dialogue with others about what Christians are called to do in our confusing times. We also need church leaders, teachers, and scholars who can attend to the many complexities of what it means to be a Christian in a world where there are powerful institutions such as the media, governments, and economic structures, and dominating ideologies such as individualism, patriarchy, racism, capitalism, and so forth. Every Christian is responsible to find appropriate ways to live in the world, but each Christian cannot be a specialist in everything needed. So the church calls leaders, teachers, and scholars who dedicate themselves to special problems that face the church as it seeks to be faithful. Bringing all our knowledge in practical theology together so that our Christian faith makes a difference in the world is the task of individuals and congregations.

> Now there are varieties of gifts, but the same Spirit. . . . God has appointed teachers. . . . [but] are all teachers? . . . for knowledge will come to an end. . . . And now faith, hope, and love abide, these three; and the greatest of these is love. (1 Cor. 12:4, 27, 29; 13:13)

LEVEL-ONE METHOD OF PRACTICAL THEOLOGY—FOR CONGREGATIONS

When we are active members of a local congregation, we engage in regular worship and hear interpretations of the Bible and its relevance for our time. Preaching and worship include constant references to the Bible and its understanding of God and human life. Over a lifetime of worship and hearing about the Bible, believers continually recommit themselves to conforming their lives to their understandings of the Bible. In this sense, we are all engaged in doing practical theology: trying to discern the attitudes, decisions, and practices that are consistent with what God wants. We are trying to practice the theology in which we believe.

But Christians are always faced with complications. The first type of complication comes because of the tension between our theology and the world. For example, if we believe that God wants us to be honest and truthful in most situations, what do we do when faced with pressure from other people or from our workplaces to be dishonest? If we believe that God cares for people who cannot care for themselves because of illness or disability, what do we do when we encounter negative stereotypes of people who seem to be undisciplined in their personal lives because of addictions or personality disorders? In such situations and many others, serious Christians try to practice their faith even when it causes problems with others. A Christian may refuse to lie when pressured by a supervisor even though it results in a demotion or loss of a job. A Christian may choose to help a family with an alcoholic parent even when others criticize us for being enablers.

In situations where we face conflicts between our faith and the values of the world, we often come back to the church community for support. Being a Christian is sometimes hard, and one of the purposes of Christian community is to provide comfort for people who suffer because of their faith. One may question, Is my suffering because of my faith, or is it because I am thinking about this situation in a wrong way? Why does it hurt so much to be a Christian, and why does my behavior affect other people in a negative way? Often we are looking for reaffirmation that what we are doing is correct, and that our attempt to be faithful Christians is worth the difficulties it creates. In fact, local congregations can celebrate with individuals who have negative experiences when they try to be faithful. Jesus was in trouble with other people throughout his adult life because he understood the nature of God and refused to compromise his integrity for the sake of social convenience. "Blessed are those who suffer for righteousness' sake" (Matt. 5:10).

Similar complications can exist on the level of the congregation itself. For example, a church community may decide that they need to engage in evangelism with the families in a new housing development. Based on their study, they find that 75 percent of the new families do not have a church home even though many of them would like to attend worship on a regular basis. The congregation might decide to engage in organized visitation to get to know the families

> How have you faced the tensions between the faith you practice and the sometimes alien values of the world?

and commit themselves to developing programs that would meet their needs. They might discover that many families in the development have preschool children who have no place to go when the parents are working. They might decide to start a preschool program and day care as a way of responding to these new families. As a result, some families might become active members who have leadership skills that could be useful in the church.

However, organizing a day-care center and preschool program is a big operation that requires money, suitable space, and trained and certified teachers. Making such a project feasible requires work and sacrifice from congregational members. In addition, the new families who come into the church may have traditions and values that are different from what the established membership is used to. One congregation I know is a mixture of European Americans, African Caribbeans, and immigrants from Belize. Designing worship services, music programs, and community-outreach programs for such a diverse group is challenging. A congregation that embarks on any program must be ready to struggle, sacrifice, and change in order to engage in effective evangelism.

A second type of complication comes to believers when the worship and the interpretation of the Bible they experience in the congregation are confusing. The leaders of local congregations are fallible human beings, and the inherited tradition has its own ambiguities. Some preachers preach a false teaching that is confusing for those who trust their leadership. What happens to believers when the received theology in a local congregation is itself distorted?

For example, most churches, until recently, taught that women could not be ordained leaders who were allowed to preach the gospel and preside over the sacraments. Many churches in the global Christian community continue to teach this kind of theology.[2] The history of ideas about gender, motherhood, and sexuality is long and complex. It is not surprising that local church leaders are confused about the new movements for gender equality and changes in marriage and family covenants. Sometimes the Bible seems to favor male leadership and expects female believers to be silent in church and submit to their husbands.[3] In a particular marriage, the husband may be comfortable with gender hierarchy and be familiar with certain biblical passages that support his position in his relationships. The wife may respond to the debates about gender equality within the church and begin to challenge her husband's views. What happens to a marriage when a husband and wife hear different interpretations of the gospel? It can result in conflict, debate, and tension that in some cases threatens the marriage itself.

Suppose that a couple comes to their pastor for marriage counseling with questions about whether the Bible says that wives should submit to their husbands. What would good practices of pastoral care be? We should remember that the pastoral leader also has opinions about what the Bible says about gender relationships that would influence her or his perspective toward this couple. She may side with the husband and encourage the wife to adapt to her husband's wishes. He may side with the wife and challenge the husband to change his viewpoint. In this case the practice of pastoral care is not just the application of psychology to the issues of marriage, but a question about the truth of the gospel. Many preachers are themselves in transition in what they believe on particular issues. Theology itself is constantly changing as we learn more about how the Bible was written and what God wants from humans. Sometimes the preached gospel is an inaccurate reflection of the will of God for believers in particular times and places. In this example, local church leaders may need to revise their understanding of the Bible in response to the problems believers confront when they try to be faithful.

In summary, at its most basic level, practical theology is the attempt of believers to practice their faith according to their understanding of the Bible and its interpretation. This practice requires disciplined and corporate thinking about what God wants from believers and how to resolve the complications of living this faith in a particular social context. Sometimes being faithful puts us in tension with other persons and our society for good reasons and we need the support and encouragement of the church to remain faithful in the face of negative consequences. Sometimes being faithful raises questions about whether the gospel we practice is true and appropriate for our lives at this time. In either case, congregations become a center of practical theological thinking as together we sort out the faithful practices of our faith. All Christians do practical theology when they try to correlate their faith with their everyday lives.

> Are you comfortable with the idea that your church sometimes preaches a false gospel?

LEVEL-TWO METHOD OF PRACTICAL THEOLOGY—FOR CHURCH LEADERS

Congregational leaders have a larger responsibility to help believers and congregations interpret the meaning of the Bible for everyday practices. This means that church leaders have to learn a method of doing practical theology that can guide the processes of theological reflection for struggling believers in their congregations. At this level, there are four essential steps to an adequate practical theological method for the local congregation: (1) reflection on practices of Christian communities; (2) reflection on the social and cultural context of practices; (3) reflection on the biblical and theological roots of practices; and (4) planning and implementing new, transforming practices for particular communities of faith.[4]

Step One: Reflection on Practices of Christian Communities

Reflection on practices is what happens when a congregation gathers for worship, study, and action in its life together. Christians are always reflecting on their attitudes and behaviors to see if they conform to the gospel as they understand it. For individuals, this process of reflection is intensified whenever there is tension or conflict. In the previous example, the wife who was challenging her husband on his views of gender was hearing two different interpretations of gender equality; she probably spent many hours thinking about this tension and seeking out new resources to help her in her quandary. Congregations engage in intensified reflection whenever there is a call to new practices or a challenge to familiar practices. In the example above, a congregation was called to reach out to the families in a new housing development because of the mandate for evangelism. But when they followed this call, they realized that they had not anticipated the complications of taking the new people seriously and the tensions of trying to integrate new people into the existing congregational culture. They were forced into a deeper kind of reflection about the gospel and the needs of everyone in the congregation and the community.

Church leaders have a responsibility to anticipate the need for intensified reflection and provide skills and resources to prepare the members for the challenges ahead. For something as basic as the congregational theology of marriage, church leaders should not wait until there is serious conflict or family crisis before addressing the changing gender expectations. Leaders need to be alert to the underlying tensions that are part of the everyday life of the faithful and help the people begin to reflect on their practices before the tensions become unmanageable. The call to evangelism is a significant part of congregational life for many members, but the full implications of following this call are not always apparent. Leaders can begin by helping congregational members reflect on their current practices of evangelism. Who do members talk to at work, school, and in local community activities? How often does a discussion of faith come up, and what do they say when they hear questions of faith from others? How comfortable are the members if they are challenged by those who have different backgrounds and values? These kinds of questions can be addressed in regular Bible study, mission study groups, prayer groups, or even standing committee meetings. If a congregation is regularly engaging in disciplined reflection about their practices of faith, then they will gain the skills they need when an important new call comes to them.

Sometimes intense theological reflection on practices comes in the form of crisis. Members may disagree about gender issues, or whether evangelism is the core mission for this congregation at this time. Groups sometimes form that begin to challenge and eventually mistrust one another. Tensions can escalate until they threaten the unity and mission of the congregation. In such a situation, church leaders should begin by facilitating a process of reflection on practices. It is often helpful to review the congregation's history and its debates on its practices. What happened before when the congregation faced conflict and tension? What were the issues and how did they get resolved? Then the leader can encourage reflection about the proposed new practices and their strengths and limitations. Through such a process, a congregation may find a way to have a shared discussion that brings them together with a larger concern for the health of the whole congregation. In some cases, polarization and alienation have already gone too far and the only solution may be compromise or separation for a time. Hopefully, the leaders will have the skills to anticipate tension and use practical theological method as a form of intervention.

Does your congregation have a regular study program to reflect on faithful practices of Christian faith?

Step Two: Reflection on the Social and Cultural Context of Practices

A second step of intensified theological reflection comes when members begin a study of the contextual issues involved in any issue or program. Church leaders need to understand the influence of the social and cultural context on the congregational members. A leader should know what kind of television programs the members are watching and what values they are hearing from the media. Movies, magazines, newspapers, books, and the Internet are powerful molders of peoples' lives, probably beyond what they are aware of themselves. For example, how many members of the church are fans of various talk shows on television and radio? What kinds of stories and analysis are they hearing. Does it make a difference whether they are fans of Oprah Winfrey, or Rush Limbaugh, or both? Does it matter if persons in the congregation are addicted to Internet pornography or regularly watch self-help psychology shows? Where do people get their images of masculinity and femininity and the proper roles of men and women in marriage and parenting?

These are complex questions and there are no easy answers. Fortunately, there are many people asking these same questions and trying to understand the culture with the tools of the modern social sciences. Local colleges and universities have regular courses on gender issues, marriage and family, and the influence of culture on individuals. The denominations have produced instructive policy statements and study guides on a variety of issues such as the family, sexuality, the role of women, and so forth. Church leaders have a responsibility to anticipate the issues that are embedded in the everyday lives of church members and prepare resources for those who need help.

The congregation that follows a call to engage in evangelism by reaching out to the families in a new housing development needs to prepare itself. How are the congregation's perceptions of cultures and values shaped by public debates on immigration policies and national security? For example, it might be good to talk to local realtors and banks in the area to find out the social class and economic status of the new families. It could make a big difference if the new development is an upscale community populated by high-level state employees. Or perhaps the new development is a project of Habitat for Humanity with affordable housing for first-time home buyers from working-class families. Using the methods of sociology, the congregation could find important information by doing surveys and reading studies done by the local government.

Depending on the initial results of this study, the congregation may need to change its strategy for approaching these families, and get some training in how to engage the families and respond to their needs. Likewise, the members need to understand their own social and cultural context and how it influences their lives and values.

Step two assumes that every Christian practice is embedded in a social and cultural context with many conflicting influences. Part of doing good practical theology is making use of the social sciences to understand the cultural context of church practices in all their complexity. What starts out as a simple call to evangelism or an interesting debate about gender turns into a complex social situation that cannot be easily understood. Fortunately, the social sciences are already organized to help us understand our cultural context better so that we have a better chance to being faithful.

> Is your congregation aware how powerful ideas such as gender, race, and class affect Christian practices?

Step Three: Reflection on the Biblical and Theological Roots of Practices

Reflecting on the Bible and its interpretation is implicit in all the other stages of practical theology because it is the identity-shaping practice of every serious Christian. Practical theology begins with a believer's wish to conform her or his practices to God in Christ as revealed in the Scriptures and interpreted by the churches. Out of these formative experiences with Scripture and tradition comes the call to practice one's faith. For example, a congregation that feels called to evangelism is enacting certain understandings of Scripture and of the church.

However, engaging in a disciplined study of practices raises new questions that require additional biblical and theological reflection. Biblical and theological questions emerge as a congregation discovers the hard work in visiting families from a different socioeconomic and cultural perspective, the complications of organizing day-care and pre-school programs, and integrating new leaders who come from other church cultures. After initial attempts to visit and form connections with the new families fail, congregational leaders may wonder if evangelism is really a genuine call of the congregation, or whether they should focus on some other program. As they face the challenges of redesigning the worship and music program to respond to different cultures, leaders may wonder whether the music they have been singing for many years is really an accurate interpretation of the Bible. Some U.S. congregations are struggling with the introduction of a contemporary worship to supplement the traditional European American focus on classical music. Other congregations wonder how to respond to immigrants who prefer a formal style of worship and are not comfortable with the less structured styles that are their current practices. Such questions eventually can drive a congregation back to a basic study of Scripture and theology. Asking, What does God want us to do? can readily raise other questions: Who is God, and what is the meaning of the love that Jesus practiced in his ministry?

Fortunately, many of the questions that will face local congregational leaders have been already studied and written about extensively. Denominations have many resources about the nature of evangelism in an intercultural world. Agencies such as The Alban Institute have books on many subjects that a local congregation might want to study.[5] Denominational and independent religious publishers have hundreds of titles by distinguished scholars and church leaders touching on many topics of current interest. The mainline denominations all require a seminary education for its ordained pastors so that they will be familiar with the many resources available when complex theological issues emerge. Congregational leaders need to be prepared in anticipation of deeper theological issues that come up in their churches. A shallow interest in evangelism is not sufficient for facing the many complicated issues of genuine evangelism with real people in the modern world.

Sometimes world events trigger the crisis that drives a congregation to deeper biblical and theological study. For example, after the 9/11 crisis, many congregations have felt called to understand the nature of Islam in the world today. Confronting interreligious issues was not high on the agenda for most U.S. congregations until confronted more directly with the dangers of interreligious conflict. Studying the texts and history of Islam necessarily drives many Christian communities back to their own texts and history

Is your congregation regularly studying new theological perspectives in order to help you grow in faith?

to understand better the conflict between Christianity and Islam. Congregational leaders need to have a method of practical theology so they know how to proceed when such crises develop.

Step Four: Planning and Implementing
New Transforming Practices for Particular Communities of Faith

Study and new understanding of practices and their social and biblical context is an important part of the method of practical theology. But the real test of practical theology is whether it leads to new practices for particular communities. There is a danger that a community will become so engaged in study and reflection that they avoid the risk and challenge of actually engaging in new practices. New insights about the nature of God and the church can be intoxicating. A believer can feel like she or he has found a new identity that is deeper than imagined at the beginning of the process. But Christian life requires more than reflection; faith requires practice. Sometimes called the "so what" question in theology, practices are the patterns of action that make salvific differences in the life of real people.

For example, for a married couple struggling with changing gender issues, it is not enough to discover foundations for the concept of gender equality in the Bible, although that can be personally liberating for many women and men. The next question is, What practices follow from this belief? In popular media, there are many controversial debates about shared housework, co-parenting, renegotiating sexual interactions, and so forth. All these issues are related to how power is enacted in a marriage within a particular context. Husbands and wives are not isolated individuals, but part of gender power structures that affect educational opportunities, economic incentives, extended family relationships, and many other issues. For church leaders, it is not enough to preach about gender equality, but hymns need to be examined for gender bias, overuse of male attributes of God needs attention, and couples need practical guidance on how to communicate differently and how to balance individual gifts and limitations with the demands of the marriage, the family, and the society. After fifty years of the feminist movement, every aspect of gender relationships is up for debate and is highly contested. Church leaders need to ask about what resources couples need to develop new practices that follow the insight that the gospel leads to gender equality within a patriarchal society.

Fortunately, there are many resources on Christian practices on which local leaders may draw. Gender equality in families and society has been considered by most denominations, and policy statements, educational materials, and reference to other resources are available. The role of leaders is to have a general familiarity with what is available and the research tools to discover exactly the right materials for a particular congregation. In a society where Oprah and Dr. Phil are giving practical advice to couples every day, church leaders need to understand the powerful influences in society and bring these ideas into dialogue with the gospel. Beyond that, couples may need disciplined covenant

Does your congregation have covenant groups to help members change their practices of faith as they grow in new understandings of the gospel?

groups that meet regularly with a commitment to talk about their relationships and be willing to examine themselves in relation to their identities as Christians. Most couples will be unable to make changes in everyday practices and resist the negative images of the culture unless they are part of disciplined groups where people pledge to be honest and open minded with other Christians. Only in such a context can changes occur that make a real difference in their lives and present models for children and other adults about the meaning of the Christian life.

APPENDIX TWO
Methods of Practical Theology
for Teachers and Scholars

In this appendix I summarize my insights and experience for the benefit of teachers and scholars who are responsible for teaching and research in practical theological thinking.

Practical theology is the academic theological discipline that studies the practices of the churches in conversation with other branches of theology and the modern social sciences and designs programs and strategies for salvation/transformation of the church and the world. Other branches of theology include biblical studies, historical studies, systematic theology, and ethical theology. The most common social sciences used in practical theology are psychology, sociology, anthropology, economics, and ecological studies. Physical sciences sometimes are influential, including biology, brain science, and environmental studies.

A BRIEF HISTORY OF PRACTICAL THEOLOGY

Christians have always been interested in the practical aspects of Christian faith and life and understand faith and practice as a unity. Edward Farley calls the unity of faith and practice a "habitus" (habit of faith) in distinction from the Enlightenment dichotomy of religion and science.[1] Modern practical theology begins with Friedrich Schleiermacher's 1811 book, *Brief Outline of the Study of Theology*,[2] which organized all theology into philosophical theology, historical theology, and practical theology. He understood practical theology as theological reflection on church practices, but focused most of his attention on the leadership of clergy. Farley criticized his perspective because it overemphasized the "clerical paradigm" rather than the full range of church practices organized by its mission in the world.[3]

Practical theology as an academic discipline is primarily a development of twentieth-century dialogue between theology and the new social sciences. First to emerge, around 1900, were professional groups, journals, and research centers in particular practices of church life: Christian education, pastoral care, homiletics, liturgics, and mission studies.[4] Since the 1940s there have been efforts to coordinate these separate guilds into shared research and the development of an integrating discipline of practical theology.[5] Since 1990, practical theologians have generated several national organizations and journals, an international academy, and an international journal.[6] From these efforts has come significant literature that creates an academic field with recognition by universities and interdisciplinary professional societies.[7] Practical theology was recently recognized as full member of the American Academy of Religion, one of the largest international meetings of religious scholars.[8] Given that practical theology is a recent development as an academic field, there are many aspects that wait for development.[9]

SIX TYPES OF PRACTICAL THEOLOGY

In 1985, Donald Miller and I developed a description of six types of practical theology, depending on one's view of the relationship of the church and the world, and depending on one's approach to the relationship of theology and science.[10] Some types of practical theology see the church and the world working in close collaboration with one another, while other types see tension or a dichotomy between church and world. For example, magisterial churches such as Roman Catholics, Lutherans in Europe, and Anglicans in England understand the church as the conscience of society, calling the state as well as individuals to be faithful to the gospel. Many Protestant churches in the United States and elsewhere insist on separation of church and society and do not expect the society to be able to live up to the demands of the gospel. Scholars in universities often prefer the term "critical correlation" to describe the relationship of church and world in practical theology.[11] By this term they mean that the church must translate its insights into language the world can understand and evaluate the merit of the church's beliefs and values by public standards. This means that the revealed gospel and the insights of secular disciplines have essentially equal opportunities to make their case and persuade others to follow their lead.

Some types of practical theology are comfortable with the methods of the social sciences and see them as entirely appropriate for study of the church and its practices. Other types are uneasy about the theology-science relationship and place them in a more antagonistic relationship. For example, there is currently much scientific research about whether religious faith plays a positive role in the mental and physical health of individuals. Some sociological and psychological studies show that persons who pray regularly, attend church regularly, and claim to have a strong personal faith are more likely to be happy, free of disease, and to live longer, healthier lives.[12] Critics raise the question of whether personal faith can be measured by self-report studies on church attendance, beliefs, and practices such as prayer, and whether religion can be understood in generic terms without reference to the particular beliefs and practices of historical traditions.[13] What is really being measured with such research methods, and what value does such research have for church life?

Critical methods include two kinds of criticism: classical scientific methods that use empirical evidence to challenge theories and critical theories that question the foundational assumptions of science. The social sciences study human behavior and community by developing hypotheses, collecting evidence, and evaluating the reliability and validity of research. Science often challenges theology by asking for evidence of how faith works in the world. Critical theories raise significant questions about the validity of scientific methods and traditional theological concepts. I am thinking here of feminist, postmodern, and postcolonial critical theories. These theories ask whether science and theology are too often identified with conserving values of the past that are implicated in oppression and whether they can serve as resources for the liberation of all of human beings. They further ask whether science and theology are capable of understanding the desires and hopes of people who have been identified as nonpersons and denied the power to shape their own destinies.[14]

Critical theories also raise questions of power and control. They suggest that studying the practices of the churches in dialogue with theology and science is not such a straightforward enterprise. Who decides what practices of the church deserve careful study? Who decides what scientific theories and methods are appropriate for understanding the world? Who decides what ideas and values from theology are normative for the practical theologian? Critical theorists ask whether practical theology is another attempt of the churches to consolidate their power and control and deny resources and freedom for the people of the world who are oppressed.[15] These are questions scholars in practical theology are called to address.

One result of questions of power is a sociopolitical understanding of practical theology. If every theology is an exercise in power, that is, an attempt to enforce particular interpretations of truth that provide benefit for certain social classes,[16] then practical theology itself is an exercise in power. Therefore, its definition, methods, and practices need to confess the power assumptions embedded in its work. Richard Osmer calls this aspect of practical theology "rhetorical strategies":

> Rhetorical strategies . . . [are] used to make a particular argument convincing to a specific group of readers or listeners on a particular occasion. These strategies include appeals to reason, emotions, examples, and the personal character or credibility of the speaker/writer.[17]

Some practical theologians argue that all practical theology is rhetorical in the sense that Osmer describes. That is, every form of research in practical theology is aimed at the exercise of power for particular goals and particular groups of people. Scholars that use critical theories are often suspicious of the scientific methods that attempt to hide their exercise of power behind objective and universal goals for the benefit of all people. Rather, they argue, all of practical theology is sociopolitical and rhetorical, not just the final steps of influencing persons and society.[18]

From a theological point one might also ask related and potentially deeper questions. For some Christians, the main goal of practical theology is to know the will of God. That is, many believers think God is active in the world, and that the fulfillment of human life comes as humans conform their lives to the will of God. As Albert Einstein supposedly once said: "I want to know God's thoughts; the rest are details."[19] Christians often believe that if we understand God's intentions and actions in relation to the world, we will be better able to live faithful and fulfilling lives. Given this assumption, a question for practical theology as a scientific discipline is, How does one study God? Is God the kind of data that can be studied like any other subject? If we study human beings in enough detail, will we be able to discern God's patterns in these details? And when we study human beings, how do we account for the existence of human evil? If evil intentions are hidden by powers and principalities and deceptive personal behaviors, even in the researchers, how can we sort out the presence of God as distinct from human desires and evil intentions? Can a scholar who wants to know the will of God find data to shape one's faith, or does one always find the truth that supports the bias of the researcher? Given the assumption of this study that God and humans are characterized by ambiguity, how can a practical theologian gain a perspective from which to engage in disciplined study? Who decides the nature of an adequate and relevant practical theology?[20] These and other questions will be addressed in the following discussion of various methods in practical theology.

DEFINITIONS OF PRACTICAL THEOLOGY

Throughout my teaching and research career, I have worked as a practical theologian. Over thirty years I have developed a variety of definitions of practical theology, depending on the research project.

1. *Scientific Definition*: "Practical theology is critical and constructive reflection within a living community about human experience and interaction, involving a correlation of the Christian story and other perspectives, leading to an interpretation of meaning and value, and resulting in everyday guidelines and skills for the formation of persons and communities."[21]

2. *Ecclesial Definition 1*: "[Practical] theology is a set of beliefs, attitudes, and behaviors motivated by the Christian gospel and practiced by Christian communities to care for all people—resources for survival and healing, trustworthy community, and empowerment for justice-work on behalf of others."[22]

3. *Ecclesial Definition 2*: "Practical theology is a sub-discipline of theology that generates theological reflection on the doctrines and practices of religious communities out of sustained attention to the suffering and hope of persons toward the goal of transforming the society."[23]

4. *Social Transformation Definition*: "Practical theology is theological interpretation of the unheard voices of personal and community life for the purpose of continual transformation of faith in the true God of love and power toward renewed ministry practice" and a transformed world.[24]

In these four definitions, my peers and I are trying to find a balance between practical theology as a scientific discipline that conducts research on the practices of the church that generates constructive theology, and a sociopolitical critique of religion and society that aims at transformation of persons and society according to the gospel.

Scientific Definitions of Practical Theology

The first of these definitions, from 1985, is a more scientific definition according to the above typology. It defines practical theology as a study of practice that includes a correlation of social scientific and theological statements for the improvement of the church in the world. It outlines six steps that can provide the basis for research projects. The essential components of practical theology are:

a. Description of lived experience

b. Critical awareness of perspectives and interests

c. Correlation of perspectives from culture and the Christian tradition

d. Interpretation of meaning and value

e. Critique of interpretations

f. Guidelines and specific plans for a particular community[25]

As a teacher I have found these six steps helpful in guiding students through numerous research projects. In most of my classes, I have asked students to follow these steps, and they have produced some amazing projects. I usually require personal, face-to-face interviews for my assignments because understanding God, the church, and the life of believers cannot depend solely on one's individual opinion and personal religious experience. God is relational, and knowledge of God's will emerges most frequently out of conversations and shared practices with other Christians. Saints and mystics of historical and contemporary times were formed in community and engaged in regular dialogue with others. They may have experienced direct revelation from God, but their ideas of God were also a result of socialization and disciplined practices within communities of believers. Students are frequently surprised when they listen carefully to the religious experiences of others. What often seems self-evident in one's own mind is quickly challenged if the faith of another is taken seriously. This is what I mean by "description of lived experience."

Being surprised by the witness of another person to the reality of God in his or her life raises questions about one's own self-awareness. What is surprising about what the other person has said? How is my experience of God different from that of others? What is blocking me from understanding this person? Do I have sin in my life that I need to examine in order to see more clearly? These can be painful questions as students realize they carry a range of assumptions about themselves and others that may not be true and which could cause harm if imposed on another using the authority of ministry. Many students decide to engage in spiritual direction or pastoral counseling as a result of their research assignments because they need to understand themselves better and experience healing before they can be effective ministers, teachers, and scholars. This is what we mean by "critical awareness of perspectives and interests."[26]

Interviews with others and engaged self-reflection increases the students' awareness of the context in which they are doing their work. The experiences they are thinking about are not just the result of individual creativity, but depend on organized and historically developed theories of interpretation. In the twenty-first century, almost everyone in the United States is shaped by the powerful social media (newspapers, magazines, books, television, advertising, music, movies, Internet, etc). We are bombarded everyday by messages about how we should think about what is going on in the world. Most scholars have received years of intense educational experiences within high-status universities. Behind these ideas are theories about the world, human beings, and God. When we become students and scholars called to leadership, we bear responsibility for understanding where formative ideas come from and what their effects are.

For example, it is not an easy task to understand modern psychology and its history over the last one hundred years. Psychology is a complex social construction with much diversity and alternative understandings of many things. When we go more deeply into psychology, we are often overwhelmed by its complexity. Part of our job as scholars is to find how our identities are shaped by powerful theories such as the psychology of our times. There are no simple solutions, because when we ignore the power of modern psychology, we often find ourselves using the very theories that we thought we had rejected.[27]

Theology is similarly complex. As "masters of divinity," we become responsible for understanding the history and interpretation of the Scriptures, the history of the churches through the ages, and the contemporary debates about the meaning of Christian life in modern times. It takes years of study to become comfortable with this body of literature and able to interact competently with mentors who have devoted their life to one aspect or another. Every understanding of the full tradition we have inherited is merely one perspective on a complex history that is beyond individual comprehension.

Theology and the social sciences are not completely separate disciplines, but have developed in dialogue with one another in recent centuries. Many of the social sciences were the creative work of religious minds trying to understand the world in which they lived. Christian assumptions are built into many of the social sciences. Yet there is a problem because the scientific method ignores or denies the existence of God, or at least defines God as something that cannot be studied by the methods of science. This has led to a certain alienation between science and religion that makes their relationship problematic. Karl Barth, for example, believed that the social sciences were influenced too much by liberal enlightenment philosophical assumptions that put them in opposition to the heart of the Christian gospel. Barth believed that the self-revelation of God was more reliable than the observations of scientists, and that science was dangerous because it placed human beings outside the reign of God. Barth's experience of the German Nazi government led him to this insight. He watched all of the major guilds of science lend their expertise to the murderous programs of genocide and war that created the Holocaust. He believed that the only cure for such human evil was submission to the will and sovereign authority of God.[28]

Barth's critique of the social sciences must be taken seriously. Some students assume too easily that their faith and modern psychology have no contradictions and that they can integrate theology and psychology in a casual way. However, practical theologians have discovered that the "correlation of perspectives from culture and the Christian tradition" is a difficult hermeneutical task. Ideas that seem similar may in fact be quite different, even contradictory. Even if one has gained competence in both social science and theology, the methods for engaging in a competent dialogue between them is very complex. Practical theologians need to become skillful in the analogies, identities, and nonidentities of the various theories of interpretation so that the results lead to creative synthesis, not just surface similarities.[29]

There is a moment of truth when the practical theologian must give an "interpretation of meaning and value." In scientific terms, this is when the scholar must make a personal commitment to one of several possible interpretations of the data collected. There is never any certainty about which of many interpretations is most correct. According to the philosophy of science, every interpretation is a matter of probability and perspective, which means that the scholar may be wrong when making any particular interpretation. There may be other ways of understanding the reality of what is studied that would be more productive of new research and knowledge. Every scholar is limited in training, skills, social location, and filled with prejudices. But the moment of truth cannot be avoided. If the scholar never gives an interpretation, then the community is left with a confusion of observations that may or may not be valid or helpful. The goal of scientific research is to discover something that is true and could lead to deeper insight and useful practical knowledge. Theologically, the moment of truth is when the practical theologian confesses, "This is true; this, I believe, is the will of God." Any scholar who is not terrified of making such a statement does not know the history of the church and the terrible human evil that has resulted from those who are overconfident that they know what God wants. But without this confession, there can be no faithfulness.

The terror of committing oneself to an interpretation of truth and value leads to the next step in the scientific method—critique of interpretation. In academic research, students are asked to describe the limitations and weaknesses of their research. How might the researcher be mistaken at each of the prior steps that could have led to a false interpretation? What are the possible flaws and limitations of this research? What further research should be done to test whether there is any truth in this research project? The rhythm of exploring human faith and life and self-critical awareness is a part of all practical research. In theological terms, there is the rhythm of confession of faith and confession of sin, which is built into Christian theology.

The final step in practical theology is developing "guidelines and specific plans for particular communities." This is the step that is distinctive from some other branches of theology—biblical studies, historical theology, and systematic theology. Each of these academic disciplines is charged with discovering what is true. What does the prophet Jeremiah think about the role of women? What was the nature of the debate about the divine-human relationship at the Council of Nicea? What did Søren Kierkegaard mean by the term *anxiety*, and how can this term help us to understand human life in the modern era?

Practical theology (and often theological ethics)[30] is responsible for "being practical." We must ask the question, What difference do these insights mean for living communities of faith and practice, and how, in detail, might these programs be faithfully carried out? For example, it is not enough for a practical theologian in education to say that the church should be more evangelistic. Such a leader must also ask, How could the church design, plan, and carry out a three-year training program for laypersons so they can share their faith more effectively with their neighbors and co-workers? There is more to education and mission than quoting the Great Commission of Matthew 28:19-20. Practical theologians also have to design programs that lead to skills (How can I talk about my faith at the hospital?), spiritual disciplines (What study guide can I use to understand evangelism better and improve my prayer life?), and communities of support (How can we help one another gain courage to share our faith in the world?).

Developing "guidelines and programs for a particular community" is a challenging task because people and congregations change slowly. There are usually reasons why a congregation is not more evangelistic and why the members are not at ease in sharing their faith with others. They may be afraid to leave the comfort of their social class and visit the Latino community near Wal-Mart. They may not want the church to grow if it includes Christians with a different denominational tradition. Rodney Hunter has said that practical theology in local congregations is more like parenting—the results take a long time and competence requires disciplined focus over many life stages to reach one's goals.[31] There are no simple answers about how a local community can be faithful in its practices.

Finally, the circle of practical theology begins again. New practices that arise from following the practical-theology method become the basis for new research. As soon as a new practice is implemented, questions about its meaning and value arise. This leads to new interviews, new self-awareness, and new correlations of culture and theology. Thus, the practical theology method is like a wheel rolling along a road. All six of the steps we have described constantly repeat themselves and interact with one another. Local communities of faith are constantly thinking about how they are practicing their faith, about their identity as Christians, about what it means to live in a particular culture, about the meaning of the gospel for their time and place. Practical theologians are those church leaders charged with understanding the scientific and theological methods and skills that are involved in the everyday practices of Christian life. As such, they are called to facilitate the faithful practices that help the community know and follow the will of God.

Ecclesial Definitions of Practical Theology

The second definition of practical theology focuses on ecclesial care. How can the church embody the care of God for all humanity and creation through "resources for survival and healing, trustworthy community, and empowerment for justice work on behalf of others"? This definition assumes that God cares for the world, and that as believers and followers of Jesus we have received a mission of care. How one develops a practical theology of care depends on one's understanding of God and the work of salvation in Jesus Christ. This definition includes particular theological assumptions about the nature of the trinitarian God and the world.

The third definition highlights the role of practical theology in assessing the function of theological concepts within living communities of faith. The role of theology is to discern the truth of the gospel in language and symbols that make sense in the changing historical situation. The cultures and philosophies that shape human life are constantly changing, and theologians are hard at work keeping up with changing culture and philosophy and, in fact, trying to influence the public debates with the gospel. Theologians make available their insights and interpretations to local communities of faith. Through sermons, books, workshops, adult study, and action programs, local communities of faith try to understand the truth and relevance of the gospel for a particular moment of life and put their beliefs into action. Their struggle to engage in faithful practices becomes a form of feedback for theologians. The role of practical theologians is to study the latest research and ideas of contemporary theologians and study the living experiences of believers and local congregations and see if there are any convergences or tensions between these two realms of Christian life.

Social Transformation Definitions of Practical Theology

The fourth definition of practical theology from 1991 takes into account the radical nature of human sin and evil and the postmodern criticism of modern science and theology because of its culpability for empires and other systems of domination in human history:[32] "Practical theology is theological interpretation of the unheard voices of personal and community life for the purpose of continual transformation of faith in the true God of love and power toward renewed ministry practice." This politicized and relational definition of practical theology leads to a different emphasis in practical theology, and puts the focus on knowing the mind and will of God within a particular sociopolitical context.

I came to this social transformation understanding of practical theology through my research in domestic and sexual violence starting in 1985. My research challenged me to develop a different understanding of the depth of human sin and renewed respect for the powerful ideologies about gender, race, and class that shape our identities as Christians. How does one engage in research on a secret like sexual violence that is protected by many layers of personal and social rationalization? Many scholars in the prevention of domestic violence movement slowly began to understand that prevention of violence against women in U.S. society requires substantial social change, not just individual insight and healing. How does a practical theologian design and carry out research that is taboo within a particular culture? How does one discover the will of God in human situations where evil dominates the imagination of most people?

My research into pastoral care in situations of sexual and domestic violence presented interesting challenges. First, domestic violence occurs in settings where an abuser regularly uses deception to ensnare his victim and hide his deeds from disclosure. His social status as parent, male, and often middle class protects his domain of power and control. Second, families and intimate relationships, especially when sexual, are considered private, secret, and protected from public disclosure by socially constructed layers of shame. Third, there is a long history of public tolerance of sexual and domestic violence because its victims, mostly women and children, have not had political power to bring their complaints to the public for review. Fourth, distorted religious ideas about gender, sexuality, and hierarchy within families contribute to the reluctance of church leaders to confront these issues.

The following discussion addresses the various steps of practical theology in light of the challenges I faced in doing research about sexual and domestic violence.

1. *Practical theological reflection begins with the presence of difference and otherness in experience.* Difference provokes thought. When persons and communities become aware of some desire that contrasts with the formation of identity, the potential contradiction requires reflection. Self-conscious lived experience is filled with the tensions of similarity and difference, and identity becomes stronger as these tensions are faced and worked through. We become enlarged spiritual persons as we face the contradictions in our lives and our social setting. Human sin often leads to a split in consciousness between good and evil that oversimplifies the reality before us. Facing the contrast of good and evil rather than projecting it onto others who are perceived as different is a road to personal transformation. This means that otherness must be preserved as a window into the depths of ultimate reality. Without difference and contrast, there can be no self-conscious experience.[33]

In my research on domestic violence, the depth of experience was unlocked in the contrast between evil and suffering on the one hand and hope on the other. As long as a survivor's life is characterized by private suffering she is blocked from the depth of her own experience. But when she acts on the latent hope in her spirit by talking with others about her suffering with benevolent companions, her life begins to change. She no longer lives in a private hell, but is empowered by relational connections with others who believe her stories and provide resources for her healing. In my work with victims and abusers, it is not the evil and suffering that is compelling, but the contrast of their pain with a resilient hope that would not die. This contrast begins to unlock the depth levels of experience for our participation and research. The depth of human experience is the data for practical theology, and experience is disclosed by seeking the contrast between human suffering and experiences of hope.

Theologically, the contrast of difference in human experience is a source of *revelation*. God is found in the details of religious experience. As we attend to the depth of our experiences, we find there the energy of healing and reconciliation. As Christians, we call this insight revelation because it comes from God's self-revelation.

2. *Practical theological reflection leads to awareness of tensions within the self.* Perception of otherness and difference in experience enables one to see that the self is a fragile construction that needs continual transformation. Researchers in practical theology learn to question previous assumptions about autonomous identity, and they begin to pay attention to the hidden desires of their own hearts. Theological reflection requires a reformulation of one's personal identity, and eventually of one's *theological anthropology* or theology of humankind.

There is a search for a self of integrity and justice in the human spirit. In my research with survivors and abusers I have found courage and hope in unlikely places. If hope can be found there, perhaps it exists in other places where evil seems predominant. The physical body can remember the truth of a survivor's life for many years when the conscious mind has forgotten. The search for an integrated self is resilient and can be a source for attachments that move toward redemption. The self is relational, that is, the intrapsychic experience of the self is formed by internalization of others through emotional cathexis. Evil enters a survivor's life through the internalization of family relationships. In the recovery process, survivors reach out to others who can stand the truth and maintain supportive relationships.

When we engage in practical theological research, we are searching not only for the truth about situations and people, but we are searching for truth that will bring healing to our own spirits. We want to find hope not only for others, but for ourselves. When our research reveals the possibility of healing for others, then it increases our expectation that such healing is available for us and all people. Hope that comes from the deep recesses of shared human experiences transforms our theological doctrine of human nature. Who can deliver us from this body of death?

(Rom. 7:34). In Christ we can never be separated from the saving power and love of God (Rom. 8:38-39).

3. *Practical theological reflection leads to awareness of tension between oppression and liberation in the institutions and ideologies of community.* Communities include some parts of experience and exclude other parts. Communities attribute power to some persons and withhold it from others. The oppression of community becomes evident in reflection on the depths of experience. Previous assumptions about community life are challenged. Reflection requires a reformulation of corporate identity, and eventually of *ecclesiology,* or theology of community.

There is a search for community in the human spirit, which is more than the sum of face-to-face interpersonal relationships. By community, we mean those institutions and ideologies that shape and control the context of human lives. Women grow up in a society where male privilege is dominant. The ideology of patriarchy gives men permission to abuse women and patriarchy protects them from accountability for their behaviors. Survivors' resilient hope for community appears dramatically in their initiative to form countercommunities for healing.

In my work in domestic violence, I have been troubled by the powerful ideologies and institutions that make some people vulnerable and protect others who abuse power. The oppression of dominant institutions and ideologies permeates the theories of the social sciences through selective funding of research and educational endeavors. I have found the critical theories of feminism, race theory, and class analysis to be most helpful to understand the positive and negative impacts of social institutions and ideologies. Negatively, patriarchy, white supremacy, and class domination make both women and men vulnerable to deprivation and violence. Positively, social institutions such as family, church, volunteer agencies, governments, and economic forces potentially can prevent violence against vulnerable people, and ideologies such as patriarchy can be challenged by new ideologies of gender, race, and class. Research in practical theology must take into account the ambiguous reality of social institutions and ideologies based on the Christian doctrine of sin and evil. Out of such reflection come new reflections on the nature of human community, what theologians call ecclesiology.

4. *Practical theological reflection leads to one's ultimate horizon, one's understanding of truth or God, and whether these truths are abusive or redemptive.* Parts of our inherited and constructed religious vision are abusive, and parts are redemptive. The complicity of religious ideas in abuse challenges our previous assumptions about basic reality and the nature of God. Reflection requires a reformulation of faith, and eventually the *doctrine of God.*

The resilient human spirit sustains its search for a God of love and justice in spite of the dominance of evil. The goal of practical theology is constructive statements about God's relation to human experience that lead to strategies of liberating action. One starts with the contrast of evil and suffering with experiences of hope. This leads to the analysis of experience and culture through the use of critical theories.[34] Then there is the moment of constructive religious interpretation. Given my research, what generalization can be made about the nature of truth, that is, the nature of God?[35]

God is like a story. Every person and group forms identity through story. But consciously remembered stories often give only an official version of the past. Stories partially distort identity in favor of the ideological restrictions of those who are dominant. Persons cannot report the latent narratives in most cases. This is one reason why the voices of oppressed groups must be heard. They are often the carriers of the stories that must be heard for the full identity of a community to be known.

In theological terms, God is the story of stories. There are deeper narratives of which we are all a part, and to which our stories relate. The human soul hopes that its own self-conscious stories will be congruent with the great stories of divine life. We want our stories to be true rather than false. But we fear that the deeper truth of our lives will destroy the pseudo-stories we have created in order to defend ourselves against nonbeing. One way to know God is to deconstruct and reconstruct our individual and collective narratives.

God is relational. The philosophical discovery of the radical interdependence of all things is a basic paradigm shift from the Enlightenment world of the imperial self and the isolated object. Everything exists in a web of interdependence. Our experience is experience of the web of reality, and our individual response to the web is our contribution to its quality in the future. The web includes the interpersonal world of persons with whom we interact on a daily basis. The web includes institutions of power that set limits on behavior and action. The web includes the structure of language and the ideologies that determine perception and identity. God is the relational web, that is, the totality of everything that exists at a particular time. To the extent that we are in the web and the web is in us, our experience is the incarnation of God. The principle of empiricism[36] means attending to the web which is God. One way to know God is to reflect on the relationships within which our lives are embedded.

God is actively involved in every moment of our experience. At the heart of experience is the process that Bernard Meland refers to as "vital immediacy."[37] Understanding God can arise from analysis of the process of immediacy. The creative urge of the human soul is a response to the divine urge. There is the flow of energy from experience to experience. There is a moment of receptivity through which relationships become internalized by the individual (sensitivity). There is a moment of freedom, of novelty, by which life is passed on to the future (creativity). Because of trauma, survivors are often hindered in their ability to attend to the vital immediacy of their lives. They need the secure and compassionate presence of other souls. As nurturing relationships gain power, survivors gain strength to trust the flow of their own experience. God is active in the midst of the process of vital immediacy. Within the movement of our own spiritual experiences, our memories of the past, and our interactions with other persons and communities, God is present. One way to know God is to reflect on the vital immediacy of our experience.

God is resilient and ambiguous. There is a resilience to human faith and life that cannot be accounted for on the human level. When everything seems lost, life goes on. Persons are lost in holocausts, but those who remember them develop divine strength and creativity to continue on. Many survivors of violence die through suicide, addictions, and murder, but other survivors tell their stories and celebrate their courage after they are gone. Abusers betray the ones they love and their true selves, but some abusers hold on to life and seek healing and restitution for their evil deeds. This resilient spirit comes from God whose love and power never cease, no matter how profound the violence and oppression. Humans experience God's resilience ambiguously because we do not understand God's ways and God's vision of the future. God takes responsibility for the evil that has been done in order to save that can be saved for the future. By attending to themes of resilience and ambiguity in our research and in ourselves, we create a sense of openness for God's self-revelation.

5. *Practical theological reflection reaches its critical point when God calls the researcher into practices of transformation and uncovers the resistance to transformation.* When God has revealed truth for a particular situation, the obstacles of human sin and social evil become apparent and intolerable. God shows what is wrong and reveals the justice that must be done. Within the Gospel narratives, this is the question of *Christology*—What transformation has been promised in the life, death, and resurrection of Jesus Christ that could become reality in this particular situation? How does the God of love and power call us to become agents of transformation as disciples of Christ?

If the goal of practical theology is personal and social transformation according to the will of God, then the moment of truth for the researcher is making a personal commitment to practices of transformation. One perennial question activists and researchers in the prevention of domestic violence movement ask is whether anything we did today will make the world safer for those who are caught in interpersonal and institutional violence.[38] We base this question on the belief that ideas have power in society, and we need to be constantly aware of the power we create with our ideas. Who benefits from our research? Whose power and influence will be diminished? Will those who suffer find resources for healing and protection from further violence? Or will those who are already vulnerable be injured further? Will those who use their power to dominate and abuse others face accountability? Or will those who have power find additional strength in the results of our work. If the power we exercise is for those who are vulnerable, there could be consequences for the researcher—possible censure, punishment, or violence—from those who feel their power in threatened. We must ask ourselves whether we are willing to risk our social position and power for the sake of those who need protection. In this sense, interpretation of the will of God is christological. God's love and power are aimed at increased sensitivity and creativity for all human beings. God in Christ challenges the destructive behaviors and consequences of human sin and evil. As researchers we have to decide if we want our work to be christological in its effects. If so, we are vulnerable to the same violence and injustice as those who are vulnerable when dominating powers engage in violence.

6. *The final step of the social transformation method of practical theology is development of spiritual and embodied practices.* Such practices can be faithful or unfaithful. In fact, they will be ambiguous. This step of the method requires a reformulation of one's professional identity and, eventually, of one's *theology of ministry.*

Transformation of persons and communities takes a long time. When we address violence that results from patriarchy, white supremacy, and class oppression, transformation is measured in generations. What kinds of programs of action and education lead us toward intergenerational change? Practical theology has responsibility for long-term planning so that unborn generations will experience the transformation we seek but will not experience.

My own ministry practice was transformed by my research into sexual and domestic violence. My focus includes:

- seeking justice with survivors of sexual violence;

- confronting perpetrators who abuse their power;

- challenging my communities to be liberating rather than oppressive;

- passionately serving and worshiping the nonabusive God of love and power.

My scholarship over many years has been directed toward practical guidelines and programs to prevent domestic violence. In previous publications, I have made suggestions for how church and society can change its practices in order to prevent violence in families and intimate relationships. In the process, I have become more aware of the resistance to transformative practices, and I have been forced to explore the resistance to change in my own life. My understandings of sin and evil have deepened. At the same time I have seen miracles occur that cannot be explained by normal human expectations. I have seen survivors become advocates for healing for other survivors, finding a strength in themselves that they did not have before. I have seen abusers turn around and seek justice and restitution in their relationships with others. I have seen communities take on projects to prevent violence that go beyond what is necessary to prevent liability and embarrassment. And I have seen reconciliation between persons that seemed impossible. I know in my heart that intergenerational change is possible and that I have been a part of something profound, the full results of which I will never see.

The early environmentalists succeeded in banning the pesticide DDT after years of struggle and bald eagles and peregrine falcons came back from the brink of extinction. Most of those early to mid-twentieth-century leaders are gone now, but the results of their work continue. More struggles to protect the environment appear every day, but the movement they started continues with energy and vision. In the same way, I believe that my work to prevent violence is part of God's larger mission that will take generations to enact. I thank God that I am able to be part of something that brings the possibility of a new future because new practices are being introduced in daily church and social life.

In the model that emphasizes the goal of social transformation, practical theology is based on an empirical and personal epistemology. We know the truth by attending to the empirical depth of experience, and by honestly reflecting on our personal relationship to God within the relational web.

My own life has been transformed as I witness the resilient hope of those whose lives have been more controlled by evil than good. I found glimpses of faith in a God of love and power. God identifies with the world so that our normal distinctions about good and evil do not apply. Whatever is evil is as much a part of God as whatever is good. Yet in the midst of this radical ambiguity there is resilient hope, a restlessness toward beauty, that cannot be suppressed. In the midst of the worst evil, God's resilient hope is ceaselessly at work. This is why the witness of slaves, Holocaust survivors, and victims of child abuse is so important. They know the truth about good and evil. They know whether there is a hope at the center of reality that cannot be destroyed by evil. Those of us with social privilege who are oversocialized and anesthetized against our own evil and suffering discover such hope only with great difficulty. We must attach ourselves to those who are truly privileged, those who have been to the bottom and have found there the source of good itself. The task of practical theology is to hear the silenced voices of truth. The voices of truth must be heard against the destructive force of ideology and religion. This is the work of justice in practical theology.

SUMMARY

In this appendix, I have reviewed some of the methods of practical theology for teachers and scholars. I have distinguished several types of practical theology, some that are scientific and academic, and some that are theological and transformative. These methods overlap because one method can lead to the other. For example, one may begin research with an academic interest in an issue but discover along the way that one is passionate for change in ways that become apparent later in the process. This happens often to students who are studying for the ministry. They discover their passion along the way when their own needs for healing match the needs of people they feel called to serve. Or, one may begin with an overriding passion for change only to discover that the change one seeks requires the discipline of academic study and the ability to form coalitions with groups who do not share one's deepest passions. The rhythm of seeking academic knowledge and transformative change is dialectical. Passion requires disciplined methods and the ability to compromise; academic rigor requires deeper passions to motivate one to do the difficult work of becoming a trusted scholar and researcher.

In this project, I have sought to bring my life work as a practical theologian into dialogue with the disciplines of biblical, historical, and systematic theology. From these efforts has come a confessional statement of faith and an extended reflection on theological meaning and value I have discovered through my ministries. I offer these reflections in a spirit of humility and courage. I am humble because I realize that every believer has her or his own witness to make and my witness has no particular priority. There are many believers who have experienced suffering and hope in ways that I have not, and who have insights to bring which go deeper into the nature of God, humanity, and the world. On the other hand, I offer my witness with courage because I believe that I have encountered the reality of God in Jesus Christ. I cannot be silent with this part of the truth that I have received. Therefore, I offer it as part of the ongoing conversation of all believers who have gone before and all those who will come after. May the ancestors bless my work, and may the unborn children come to know God in Christ in their own way so they can face the challenges of the vital immediacy in their own time.

Notes

INTRODUCTION

1. See James N. Poling and Donald E. Miller, *Foundations for a Practical Theology of Ministry* (Nashville: Abingdon, 1985), for an early attempt to define practical theology.

2. See articles and reviewed books in *The International Journal of Practical Theology* (Berlin: Walter De Gruyter, since 1997), http://www.degruyter.de/journals/ijpt/.

3. I am thinking here of Karl Barth's objections to seeking revelation by using social-science methods to study human communities. He believed that revelation about God comes only through God's self-revelation and not through human effort to seek God. Karl Barth, *The Humanity of God* (Louisville: Westminster John Knox, 1996 [c. 1960]).

4. *The Book of Order: The Constitution of the Presbyterian Church (USA) 2007–2009* (Louisville: Office of the General Assembly), G 2.0200, 31.

5. For those readers who need an introduction to process theology, I refer you to the Web site for The Center for Process Studies in Claremont, California, http://www.ctr4process.org/, accessed February 25, 2011; and to the introductions by C. Robert Mesle, *Process Theology: A Basic Introduction* (St. Louis: Chalice, 1993), and by John Cobb and David Ray Griffin, *Process Theology: An Introductory Exposition* (Philadelphia: Westminster, 1976). For a more in-depth exploration, see John B. Cobb Jr., *A Christian Natural Theology,* 2d ed. (Louisville: Westminster John Knox, 2007).

6. I have been engaged in pastoral counseling, accompaniment, and advocacy with survivors and abusers of domestic violence since 1985.

7. I am thinking here of the Christian mystics during the Middle Ages, the Reformers of the Protestant Reformation, the utopian religious groups of the nineteenth century, the Pentecostals of the twentieth century, and many others.

8. The Anabaptists were Protestant Reformers in Europe during the sixteenth century who promoted adult baptism, pacifism, and radical discipleship. They were rejected by the core leaders of the Reformation: Luther, Calvin, and Zwingli. The Mennonites are their most direct descendants. The Pietists were Protestant Reformers in Europe and the United States during the eighteenth century. The Methodists, Brethren, and Baptists are their most direct descendants.

CHAPTER 1

1. "Our Father in heaven . . ."; Matt. 6:9 and parallels.

2. Whether God created the world from chaos or *ex nihilo*, from nothing, is beyond the scope of this discussion. Genesis allows either interpretation.

3. Walter Brueggemann, *The Message of the Psalms: A Theological Commentary* (Minneapolis: Augsburg, 1985).

4. *The Psalter* (Chicago: Liturgical Training Publications, 1995), 138.

5. I am thinking here of violence among David's children such as the rape of Tamar and the murder of Amnon in 2 Samuel 13.

6. Council of Chaldea, 451 C.E.: "Jesus Christ . . . truly God and truly man . . . two natures, without confusion, without change, without division, without separation."

7. There is some difference among process thinkers about the relationship of Creativity and God; Loomer, for example, believes that Creativity and God are the same. See William Dean and Larry Axel, eds., *The Size of God: The Theology of Bernard Loomer in Context* (Macon, Ga.: Mercer University Press, 1987).

8. For commentary on this passage see James Newton Poling, *The Abuse of Power: A Theological Problem* (Nashville: Abingdon, 1991). Many feminist scholars have written on this text, including Phyllis Trible, *Texts of Terror: Literary-Feminist Readings of Biblical Narratives, Overtures to Biblical Theology* (Philadelphia: Fortress Press, 1984); Pamela Cooper-White, *The Cry of Tamar: Violence Against Women and the Church's Response* (Minneapolis: Fortress Press, 1995); and others.

9. In the *HarperCollins Study Bible* (San Francisco: HarperCollins, 1993), the story of Susanna is preserved in the section on the Apocrypha under the heading: "Susanna (Chapter 13 of the Greek version of Daniel)," 1637–1640.

10. For further discussion of the Bible and violence against women, see Cheryl B. Anderson, *Women, Ideology, and Violence: Critical Theory and the Construction of Gender in the Book of the Covenant and the Deuteronomic Law* (New York: T&T Clark, 2004).

11. Catherine Mowry LaCugna, *God for Us: The Trinity and Christian Life* (San Francisco: HarperSanFrancisco, 1973).

12. This is the central question addressed by Paul Tillich in his *Systematic Theology*, 3 vols. (Chicago: University of Chicago Press, 1973–76).

13. One of the best commentaries on the problem of love in classical theology is Daniel Day Williams, *The Spirit and the Forms of Love* (New York: Harper & Row, 1968).

14. Bernard Loomer, "Two Conceptions of Power," *Process Studies* 6, no. 1 (Spring 1976), 28.

15. Linda Crockett, *The Deepest Wound: How a Journey to El Salvador Led to Healing from Mother-Daughter Incest* (New York: Writer's Showcase, 2001).

16. Alfred North Whitehead, *Process and Reality: An Essay in Cosmology*, corrected ed., ed. David Ray Griffin and Donald W. Sherburne (New York: Free Press, 1978 [1929]), 21.

17. Bernard M. Loomer, "The Free and Relational Self," in W. W. Schroeder and Gibson Winter, eds., *Belief and Ethics* (Chicago: Center for the Scientific Study of Religion, 1978), 71.

18. Robert J. Langs, *Technique of Psychoanalytic Psychotherapy, Vol. 1: Initial Contact: Theoretical Framework, Understandings the Patient's Communications, Therapist's Interventions* (New York: Jason Aronson, 1989), and other books.

19. Dean and Axel, eds., *The Size of God*, 46; and Loomer, "Two Conceptions of Power," 26: "As Reinhold Niebuhr has reminded us, through all the ironies and strange turnings of the human spirit there persists the ineradicable dialectical condition wherein every advance makes possible greater destructiveness, and every gain brings new opportunities and larger temptations."

20. American Psychiatric Association, *Diagnostic and Statistical Manual of Mental Disorders (DSM-IV-TR)*, 4th ed. (Text Revision) (Washington, D.C.: American Psychiatric Association, 2000). See also Judith Herman, *Trauma and Recovery* (New York: Basic, 1997).

21. Herman, in *Trauma and Recovery*, has one of the most cogent accounts of this vacillation between extremes of patients with PTSD and a description of the process of healing that moves toward acceptance of ambiguity.

CHAPTER 2

1. Daniel Day Williams, *The Spirit and the Forms of Love* (New York: Harper & Row, 1968), 130; edited for the sake of inclusive language.

2. William K. Frankena, *Ethics*, 2d ed. (New York: Prentice-Hall, 1988).

3. Tzu-Kung asked: "Is there a single word which can be a guide to conduct throughout one's life?" The Master replied: "It is perhaps the word 'shu' [reciprocity]: Do not impose on others what you yourself do not desire?" Confucius, *The Analects* (New York: Penguin, 1979), XV.24, 135.

4. Bernard Loomer, "Two Conceptions of Power," *Process Studies* 6, no. 1 (Spring 1976): 15. For a similar perspective, see Ted Peters, *Sin: Radical Evil in Soul and Society* (Grand Rapids: Eerdmans, 1994), and Marjorie Suchocki, *The Fall To Violence: Original Sin in Relational Theology* (New York: Continuum, 2004).

5. James N. Poling, "A Theological Integration of the Social and Personal in Pastoral Care and Counseling: A Process View," unpub. diss., Claremont School of Theology (1980), 34. See also James Newton Poling, *Deliver Us From Evil: Resisting Racial and Gender Oppression* (Minneapolis: Fortress Press, 1996), and Emilie Townes, ed., *A Troubling in My Soul: Womanist Perspectives on Evil and Suffering* (Maryknoll, N.Y.: Orbis, 1993).

6. Ibid., 36.

7. Loomer, "Two Conceptions of Power."

8. Poling, "A Theological Integration," 60.

9. Ibid., 95, 97. The reality of evil comes about partly because every advance in the power of good brings new possibilities, some of which are evil. As Bernard Loomer said, "[Niebuhr's] insight that every advance in goodness brings with it the possibility of greater evil entails the caveat that there is no progressive conquest of evil. On the contrary, the forms of destruction or diminution take on a character and a strength that are proportional to the character and strength of the advance. In this fashion every creative advance may give rise to its contrary or to some condition that either negates or qualifies the advance." William Dean and Larry Axel, eds., *The Size of God: The Theology of Bernard Loomer in Context* (Macon, Ga.: Mercer University Press, 1987), 46.

10. James Newton Poling, *Deliver Us from Evil: Resisting Racial and Gender Oppression* (Minneapolis: Fortress Press, 1996), 110.

11. For a longer discussion of this issue, see the chapters on Christology, below.

12. Rosemary Radford Ruether, ed., *Religion and Sexism: Images of Woman in Jewish and Christian Traditions* (Eugene, Ore.: Wipf & Stock, 1998).

13. Paul Kivel, personal conversation, see his Web page for other programs he has organized at http://www.paulkivel.com, accessed February 28, 2011.

14. For an insightful review of memory and Jesus, see Flora Keshgegian, *Redeeming Memories: A Theology of Healing and Transformation* (Nashville: Abingdon, 2000).

15. Williams, *Spirit and Forms of Love*, 153.

16. James N. Poling, *The Abuse of Power: A Theological Problem* (Nashville: Abingdon, 1991), 77. As far as I know, this term was first used by Daniel Paul Schreber, *Memoirs of My Mental Illness* (London: Wm Dawson and Sons, 1955 [1903]), and quoted by Sigmund Freud in *The Schreber Case* (New York: Penguin Classics, 2003 [1911]).

17. Alfred North Whitehead, *Adventures of Ideas* (New York: Free Press, 1967).

CHAPTER 3

1. "People of the land" is the English translation of *am ha-aretz*, Hebrew for the common people of ancient Israel.

2. I first heard the term "just in case" in Nicaragua, but later I realized that it describes the faith of many people who are confused by the conflicts between the many religious groups.

3. For a review of these theories from a feminist perspective, see Darby Ray, *Deceiving the Devil: Atonement, Abuse, and Ransom* (Cleveland: Pilgrim, 1998), 118ff. See also James N. Poling, *The Abuse of Power: A Theological Problem* (Nashville: Abingdon, 1991), 166–73; Joanne Carlson Brown and Carole R. Bohn, eds., *Christianity, Patriarchy, and Abuse* (Cleveland: Pilgrim, 1989); and Rita Nakashima Brock and Rebecca Parker, *Proverbs of Ashes: Violence, Redemptive Suffering, and the Search for What Saves Us* (Boston: Beacon, 2001).

4. Marit Trelstad, "Introduction: The Cross in Context," in Marit Trelstad, ed., *Cross Examinations: Readings on the Meaning of the Cross Today* (Minneapolis: Fortress Press, 2006), 1.

5. Larraine Frampton, "Good News for Modern Man, Bad News for Modern Women," in *Night Colors*, unpub. D.Min. diss., Colgate Rochester Divinity School, (1992). Used with permission of the author.

6. Wonhee Anne Joh, *Heart of the Cross: A Postcolonial Christology* (Louisville: Westminster John Knox, 2006), 71.

7. I am using "feminist" here as an inclusive term for all the global reform movements aimed at challenging patriarchy and bringing gender equity. Feminist in this usage includes womanist, *mujerista*, and other cultural terms.

8. Marie Fortune, *Sexual Violence: The Sin Revisited* (Cleveland: Pilgrim, 2005), 109.

9. Rita Nakashima Brock and Rebecca Parker, *Saving Paradise*.

10. Translation by Jim Poling, in Jacquelyn Grant, *White Women's Christ, Black Women's Jesus* (Atlanta: Scholars, 1989), 213; quoted from Harold A. Carter, *The Prayer Tradition of Black People* (Valley Forge: Judson, 1976), 49. Actual quote: "Come to we, dear Massa Jesus. De sun, he hot too much, de road am dat long and boggy (sandy) and we ain't got no buggy for send and fetch Ooner. But Massa, you 'member how you walked dat hard walk up Calvary and ain't weary but tink about we all dat way. We know you ain't weary for to come to we. We pick out de torns, de prickles, de brier, de backslidin' and de quarrel and de sin out of you path so dey shan't hurt Ooner pierce feet no more."

11. Kelly Brown Douglas, *The Black Christ* (Maryknoll, N.Y.: Orbis, 1994), 2.

12. Delores Williams, "Black Women's Surrogacy Experience and the Christian Notion of Redemption," in Trelstad, ed., *Cross Examinations*, 32. See also Delores Williams, *Sisters in the Wilderness: The Challenge of Womanist God-Talk* (Maryknoll, N.Y.: Orbis, 1993); and Grant, *White Women's Christ and Black Women's Jesus.*

13. JoAnne Marie Terrell, "Our Mother's Gardens: Rethinking Sacrifice," in Trelstad, ed., *Cross Examinations*, 49. See also JoAnne Terrell, *Power in the Blood? The Cross in the African American Experience* (Maryknoll, N.Y.: Orbis, 1998).

14. Sharon G. Thornton, *Broken Yet Beloved: A Pastoral Theology of the Cross* (St. Louis: Chalice, 2002), 115. See Douglas John Hall, *Confessing the Faith: Christian Theology in a North American Context* (Minneapolis: Fortress Press, 1996); and Dorothee Soelle, *Theology for Skeptics: Reflections on God*, trans. Joyce L. Irwin (Minneapolis: Fortress Press, 1995).

15. Thornton, *Broken Yet Beloved*, 108.

16. Chung Hyun Kyung, *Struggle to Be the Sun Again: Introducing Asian Women's Theology* (Maryknoll, N.Y.: Orbis, 1992), 57.

17. Ibid.,117.

18. Ibid., 116–17. See James N. Poling, "The Cross and Male Violence," in Trelstad, *Cross Examinations*, 50–62.

19. Edwina Sandy's sculpture of the crucified woman, *Christa* (1974), has been displayed in the Church of St. John the Divine in New York City, and other places; http://www.brooklynmuseum.org/eascfa/feminist_art_base/gallery/EdwinaSandys.php?i=2206, accessed February 28, 2011.

20. Deanna A. Thompson, "Becoming a Feminist Theologian of the Cross," in Trelstad, ed., *Cross Examinations*, 76–90.

21. Kathryn Tanner, *Jesus, Humanity, and the Trinity: A Brief Systematic Theology* (Minneapolis: Fortress Press, 2001).

22. Ibid., 30.

23. Ibid.
24. Ibid., 93–94.

CHAPTER 4

1. James N. Poling, "A Theological Integration of the Social and Personal in Pastoral Care and Counseling: A Process View," unpub. diss., Claremont School of Theology (1980), 60.

2. Bernard Meland, "Attachment to Life," unpublished lecture, Center for Process Studies, Claremont, Calif.: "In the experience of modern man, *attachment to life* manifests itself in our experience of oneness with the universe, in the feeling of the *will to live*, and in the recognition of our *organic relations* with all things. In *empirical philosophies of religion*, this attachment to life, the feeling of oneness with reality, implies a vital integration with the sustaining environment, a commitment to living processes, and an acceptance of these processes as an experienced good."

3. Bernard M. Loomer, "Two Kinds of Power," *Criterion* 15 (1976): 28.

4. Kathryn Tanner, *Jesus, Humanity, and the Trinity: A Brief Systematic Theology* (Minneapolis: Fortress Press, 2001).

5. "Within the conception of power as relational, size is fundamentally determined by the range of intensity of internal relationships one can help create and sustain. The largest size is exemplified in those relationships whose range exhibits the greatest compatible contrasts, contrasts which border on chaos (Whitehead). The achievement of the apex of size involves sustaining a process of transforming incompatible contrasts or contradictions into compatible contrasts, and of bearing those contrasts within the integrity of one's individuality." Loomer, "Two Kinds of Power," 28.

6. "Jesus' message was both political and religious at the same time: a call to repentance, a challenge to corrupt institutions and authorities, and a compassionate action directed toward the neglected and victimized of his day. He was indeed concerned with the eschatological new age to come, but in his context this meant no lack of realism as regards the actual historical situation of his people." Bernard Meland, quoting Amos Wilder, in *The Realities of Faith* (New York: Oxford University Press, 1962), 259.

7. "Jesus revealed the nature of relational power, . . . a persistent and spirit-testing commitment to the specific processes of life, . . . a discerning immersion in what is most deeply present at hand and concretely at work in our midst. . . . The discipline of this way of life involves the most mature sensitivity to the workings of concrete processes in the context of internal relations." William Dean and Larry Axel, eds., *The Size of God: The Theology of Bernard Loomer in Context* (Macon, Ga.: Mercer University Press, 1987), 17. "Faith is the willingness to attach oneself to the concrete processes of life in spite of the ambiguity which is present there. Jesus is the model of one who was able to sustain deeply internal relationships with individuals and societies in spite of great incompatibilities. Those who live in faith are called to risk following the example of Jesus-in attempting to sustain deeply internal relationships with others, and to struggle with courage to harmonize the deep contrasts found there, even the contrast between love and hate." Poling, "A

Theological Integration of the Social and Personal in Pastoral Care and Counseling: A Process View." unpub. PhD diss., Claremont School of Theology, 1979, 103–4.

8. Catherine Mowry LaCugna, *God for Us: The Trinity and Christian Life* (San Francisco: HarperSanFrancisco, 1973); Tanner, *Jesus, Humanity, and the Trinity.*

9. The following section is adapted from Poling, "A Theological Integration," 89–92, based on insights from Loomer, in Dean and Axel, eds., *The Size of God.*

10. Dean and Axel, eds., *The Size of God,* 48.

11. Ibid.

12. Ibid., 51.

13. Ibid., 53.

14. Ibid., 54.

15. Ibid., 55.

16. Ibid., 46.

17. Ched Myers, *Binding the Strong Man* (Maryknoll, NY: Orbis, 1988), 129.

18. I am thinking here of the "Left Behind" series of novels by Tim LaHaye and Jerry Jenkins, stories about the apocalypse just before Jesus' return to earth in which righteous persons left behind by the rapture defend themselves against the enemies of Christ. The extreme situation is used as a rationalization for many forms of evil that are illegal in normal times in most societies.

19. Peter was probably advocating for salvation for non-Jews, i.e., those outside the law and possibly Romans.

20. Bernard E. Meland, "The Perception of Goodness," *The Journal of Religion* 32, no. 1 (January 1952): 47–55. Philip Clayton writes, "We believe we see in the natural world an open-ended process of increasing complexity, which leads to qualitatively new forms of existence." "The Emergence of Spirit," http://clayton. ctr4process.org/files/papers/EmergenceOfSpirit.pdf, accessed February 9, 2009, 2.

21. "Purity of religious perception consists precisely in this capacity to perceive goodness in the complexity of events where evil abounds. It is not an act of ignoring evil, or of ignoring the power of evil, but an act of realistically holding in view, under vivid contrast, both good and evil as they operate in concrete events. The resolution of the conflict between good and evil is not wholly the work of man; nor is it wholly in his hands. This raises the troublesome question as to how far and in what sense men may fight the evil they apprehend and fight for the good which they cherish. One who makes an easy resolution of this problem will be overlooking the creative character of events as well as the ambiguity of men's valuations and affections. In a creative situation, good and evil intermingle, often to the human perspective in indistinguishable form. The ambiguity here arises from the tension between novel and persisting value and from the differences in the way men assess the claims of novelty and of persistent events. Creativeness demands an interrelating of these facets of meaning; but only the creative act itself can effect the transition through which interrelation occurs. The habits and fixations of men tend to line them up on one or the other side, impelling them either to a stubborn resistance toward novelty or to a championing of novelty for its own sake, thus countenancing ruthlessness toward all created goods." Meland, "The Perception of Goodness," 53.

22. Thieleman J. Van Bragt, *Martyrs Mirror: The Story of Seventeen Centuries of Christian Martyrdom from the Time of Christ to AD 1660*, trans. Joseph F. Sohm (Scottdale, Pa.: Herald, 2001).

23. René Girard, *Violence and the Sacred* (Baltimore: Johns Hopkins University Press, 1979).

24. Paul Ricoeur, *The Symbolism of Evil* (Boston: Beacon, 1986), 33.

25. Loomer, "Two Kinds of Power," 28.

26. Karen's story in her own words is found in James N. Poling, *The Abuse of Power: A Theological Problem* (Nashville: Abingdon, 1991), 35–48.

27. For more on forgiveness, see James Newton Poling, *Understanding Male Violence: Pastoral Care Issues* (St. Louis: Chalice, 2003), 189–94. See also Joretta Marshall and Marie Fortune, eds., *Forgiveness and Abuse: Jewish and Christian Reflections* (New York: Haworth, 2002); Joretta Marshall, *How Can I Forgive? A Study of Forgiveness* (Nashville: Abingdon, 2005); and John Patton, *Is Human Forgiveness Possible: A Pastoral Care Perspective* (Nashville: Abingdon, 1985).

28. Daniel Day Williams, *The Spirit and the Forms of Love* (New York: Harper & Row, 1968), 185–87. Atonement as reconciliation has four phases that are revealed in the work of Jesus and which continue in the world today. First is the disclosure of the truth of brokenness and alienation in the world (truth telling). The second phase of reconciliation is loyalty and suffering (empathy and solidarity). Third is the restoration of language as an instrument of forgiveness between persons. The fourth phase of reconciliation is the creation of a new community.

29. Linda Crockett, *The Deepest Wound: How a Journey to El Salvador Led to Healing from Mother-Daughter Incest* (New York: Writer's Showcase, 2001).

30. Judith Herman, *Trauma and Recovery* (New York: Basic, 1992).

31. Anne Wonhee Joh, *Heart of the Cross: A Postcolonial Christology* (Louisville: Westminster John Knox, 2006).

32. Jürgen Moltmann, *The Crucified God: The Cross of Christ as the Foundation and Criticism of Christian Theology*, trans. R. A. Wilson and John Bowden (Minneapolis: Fortress Press, 1993 [1974]).

33. Tanner, *Jesus, Humanity, and the Trinity*, 30.

CHAPTER 5

1. The following is an adaptation from James Newton Poling, *Render Unto God: Economic Vulnerability, Family Violence, and Pastoral Theology* (St. Louis: Chalice, 2002), chap. 13.

2. Jürgen Moltmann, *The Spirit of Life: A Universal Affirmation*, trans. Margaret Kohl (Minneapolis: Fortress Press, 1992), 7–8. See also Miroslav Volf and Michael Welker, eds., God's Life in Trinity (Minneapolis: Fortress Press, 2006).

3. Bernard Eugene Meland, *The Realities of Faith: The Revolution in Cultural Forms* (New York: Oxford University Press, 1962).

4. Catherine Mowry LaCugna, *God for Us: The Trinity and Christian Life* (San Francisco: HarperSanFrancisco, 1973), 2.

5. Ibid., 260, 288ff.

6. Kathryn Tanner, *Economy of Grace* (Minneapolis: Fortress Press, 2005), 72–85.

7. Some parts of this chapter have been previously published in "Toward a Constructive Practical Theology: A Process Theology Perspective," *International Journal of Practical Theology* 13, No. 2,199–216 (June 2010).

8. Poling, *Render Unto God*, 201.

9. Daniel Day Williams, *The Spirit and the Forms of Love* (New York: Harper & Row, 1968), 3; emphasis added and text adapted to reflect inclusive language.

10. Rosemary Radford Ruether, *Gaia and God: An Ecofeminist Theology of Earth Healing* (San Francisco: HarperSanFrancisco, 1994).

11. COSA, Committee of Support and Accountability, is a model program for sex offenders developed by Mennonite prison chaplains in Canada. More information is available on their Web site, https://www.facebook.com/pages/Circles-of-Support-and-Accountability/259099931540, or by contacting the Correctional Service of Canada Chaplaincy office at 613-996-9580. See also Correctional Service of Canada, *Circles of Support and Accountability: A Guide to Training Potential Volunteers—Training Manual* (Ottawa: self-published, 2002). For another version of this program, see Minnesota Department of Corrections http://www.corr.state.mn.us/volunteer/mncosa.htm, both accessed March 21, 2011.

12. James N. Poling, "The Theological Integration of the Social and Personal in Pastoral Care and Counseling: A Process View," unpub. PhD diss., Claremont School of Theology (1980), 60, 71.

13. Bernard M. Loomer, "Two Kinds of Power," *Criterion* 15 (1976): 28.

14. There are limits to inclusivity as a single norm. This problem has become clear in recent decades when people of privilege use inclusivity maliciously to challenge the inclusion of marginalized others because their own privilege is decreased.

15. Consider these statements from the Constitution of the Presbyterian Church, USA: D-1.0102, "Power Vested in Christ's Church. The power that Jesus Christ has vested in his Church, a power manifested in the exercise of church discipline, is one for building up the body of Christ, not for destroying it, for redeeming, not for punishing. It should be exercised as a dispensation of mercy and not of wrath so that the great ends of the Church may be achieved, that all children of God may be presented faultless in the day of Christ." G-4.0301i, "Governing bodies possess whatever administrative authority is necessary to give effect to duties and powers assigned by the Constitution of the church." G-4.0301f, "A higher governing body shall have the right of review and control over a lower one and shall have power to determine matters of controversy upon reference, complaint, or appeal." Office of the General Assembly, Louisville, 2006, http://www.pcusa.org/oga/constitution.htm, accessed March 2, 2011.

16. Poling, "A Theological Integration," 71.

17. James Newton Poling, *Deliver Us from Evil: Resisting Racial and Gender Oppression* (Minneapolis: Fortress Press, 1996).

18. Karl Barth, *Church Dogmatics*, III/3, trans. G. W. Bromiley and R. J. Ehrlich (Edinburgh: T & T Clark, 1960), 289–97.

19. Marjorie Suchocki, *The End of Evil: Process Eschatology in Historical Context* (Albany: State University of New York Press, 1988), 61.

20. Ched Myers, *Binding the Strong Man: A Political Reading of Mark's Story of Jesus* (Maryknoll, N.Y.: Orbis, 1988).

21. William Dean and Larry E. Axel, eds., *The Size of God: The Theology of Bernard Loomer in Context* (Macon, Ga.: Mercer University Press, 1987), 47.

22. For application of Emmanuel Lévinas's philosophy to the issues of sex offenders, see David Livingston, *Healing Violent Men: A Model for Christian Communities* (Minneapolis: Fortress Press, 2001).

23. Bernard Meland, *Fallible Forms and Symbols: Discourses on Method in a Theology of Culture* (Philadelphia: Fortress Press, 1976), 151.

24. Tyron Inbody, *The Constructive Theology of Bernard Meland: Postliberal Empirical Realism* (Atlanta: Scholars, 1995), 196. According to Inbody, Meland and Loomer disagree about where to locate God—whether God is identified with the multiple possibilities within Creativity, or the whole of Creativity itself.

25. "Overall, black men had an incarceration rate of 3,042 per 100,000 black men in the United States at year-end 2006 (See Appendix table 8). About 1 in every 33 black men was a sentenced prisoner. For white men, the incarceration rate for 2006 was 487 per 100,000 (or about 1 in every 205 white men). For Hispanic men, the rate was 1,261 per 100,000 (or 1 in every 79 Hispanic men)." http://bjs.ojp. usdoj.gov/content/pub/ascii/p06.txt, accessed March 11, 2011.

26. Dean and Axel, eds., *The Size of God*, 41.

27. Ibid., 51.

28. Iris Murdoch is a British philosopher and novelist for whom ambiguity is a central theme in both her fiction and nonfiction. See her books *A Fairly Honorable Defeat* (New York: Viking, 1970) and *The Sovereignty of Good* (London: Routledge, 2001) as examples.

CHAPTER 6

1. Marjorie Suchocki, "Spirit in and Through the World," in Joseph Bracken and Marjorie Suchocki, eds., *Trinity in Process: A Relational Theology of God* (New York: Continuum, 2005), 178.

2. This is a favorite quotation by African American minister, politician, and activist Jesse Jackson.

3. "Between December 1937 and March 1938 one of the worst massacres in modern times took place. Japanese troops captured the Chinese city of Nanjing and embarked on a campaign of murder, rape and looting. Thousands of bodies were buried in ditches. Based on estimates made by historians and charity organisations in the city at the time, between 250,000 and 300,000 people were killed, many of them women and children." British Broadcasting Corporation, April 11, 2005, http://news.bbc.co.uk/2/hi/223038.stm, accessed on March 21, 2011.

4. I write this essay on hope as an empirical practical theologian. I follow the lead of Bernard Loomer in my belief that knowledge is derived from physical experience. "The general empirical principle [is] that knowledge is derived from and confirmed by physical experience. This entails the notion that ideas are primarily reflective of physical or bodily experience, although they may also be elicited secondarily from other ideas that in turn are ultimately rooted in physical experience." William Dean and Larry Axel, eds., *The Size of God: The Theology of Bernard Loomer in Context* (Macon, Ga.: Mercer University Press, 1987), 24.

5. This material is an adaptation of insights from Ched Myers, *Binding the Strong Man: A Political Reading of Mark's Story of Jesus* (Maryknoll, N.Y.: Orbis, 1988), 80–87.

6. Ibid., 80–82.

7. Ibid., 82–83.

8. ". . . we are, first, commanded to survive as Jews, lest the Jewish people perish. We are commanded, second, to remember in our very guts and bones the martyrs of the Holocaust, lest their memory perish. We are forbidden, thirdly, to deny or despair of God, however much we may have to contend with him or with belief in him, lest Judaism perish. We are forbidden, finally, to despair of the world as the place which is to become the kingdom of God, lest we help make it a meaningless place in which God is dead or irrelevant and everything is permitted. To abandon any of these imperatives, in response to Hitler's victory at Auschwitz, would be to hand him yet other, posthumous victories." Emil Fackenheim, *The Jewish Return into History: Reflections in the Age of Auschwitz and a New Jerusalem* (New York: Schocken, 1978), 23–24. See also idem, *To Mend the World: Foundations of Post-Holocaust Jewish Thought* (Bloomington: Indiana University Press, 1994); and idem, "The 614th Commandment," in *Holocaust: Religious & Philosophical Implications,* ed. John K. Roth and Michael Berenbaum (New York: Paragon House, 1989).

9. Delores Williams, *Sisters in the Wilderness: The Challenge of Womanist God-Talk* (Maryknoll, N.Y.: Orbis, 1993).

10. Vincent Harding, *There Is a River: The Black Struggle for Freedom in America* (New York: Vintage, 1983), 179–94.

11. This is the text of the 1990 Annual Gandhi Lecture for the International Association of Gandhian Studies, delivered at the University of Virginia at Charlottesville on October 2, 2010, http://www.markshep.com/nonviolence/Myths.html, accessed March 2, 2011. See Mark Shepard, *Mahatma Gandhi and His Myths: Civil Disobedience, Nonviolence, and Satyagraha in the Real World* (Los Angeles: Shepard, 2002).

12. Myers, *Binding the Strong Man,* 59.

13. See Andrzej Wajda's movie *Ashes and Diamonds* for a sympathetic portrayal of one of these assassins. *Ashes and Diamonds* (Polish: *Popiół i diament*) is a 1948 novel by the Polish writer Jerzy Andrzejewski; in 1958 Wajda adapted it into a film of the same name. http://en.wikipedia.org/wiki/Ashes_and_Diamonds, accessed March 2, 2011.

14. Myers, *Binding the Strong Man,* 85.

15. Ibid., 86.

16. Ibid., 87.

17. Catherine Keller, *God and Power: Counter-Apocalyptic Journeys* (Minneapolis: Fortress Press, 2005), 136.

18. I have borrowed this word from Catherine Keller, ibid., xii: "Always between-the-times, Christian theology here works to come to terms with its own chronic imperial condition. It does not pretend to transcend its global space. It practices an alternative creativity within the interstices of empire. . . . I invoke the radical relationality from which we may construct, within the chaotic potentiality

of democracy, a coalitional politics of love." See also, Roland Faber, *God as Poet of the World: Exploring Process Theologies* (Louisville: Westminster John Knox, 2008).

19. Myers, *Binding the Strong Man*, 85.

20. David Carter, *Stonewall: The Riots That Sparked the Gay Revolution* (New York: St. Martin's, 2004).

21. James Newton Poling, *Render Unto God: Economic Vulnerability, Family Violence, and Pastoral Theology* (St. Louis: Chalice, 2002).

22. The World Bank and the International Monetary Fund were founded at Bretton Woods, New Hampshire, in 1944, to monitor international trade and global investments.

23. John B. Cobb Jr., *Sustaining the Common Good: A Christian Perspective on the Global Economy* (Cleveland: Pilgrim, 1994); and idem, *The Earthist Challenge to Economism: A Theological Critique of the World Bank* (New York: St. Martin's, 1999).

24. The Conservation Fund, 1655 N. Fort Myer Drive, Suite 1300, Arlington, VA 22209-2156, http://www.conservationfund.org/gozero, accessed March 2, 2011.

25. Poling, *Render Unto God*, chap. 14.

26. Andrea Smith, *Conquest: Sexual Violence and American Indian Genocide* (Boston: South End, 2005).

27. Catherine Keller, Michael Nausner, and Mayra Rivera, eds., *Postcolonial Theologies: Divinity and Empire* (St. Louis: Chalice, 2004); Kwok Pui-Lan, ed., *Postcolonialism, Feminism, and Religious Discourse* (New York: Routledge, 2002).

28. John B. Cobb Jr., *Christ in a Pluralistic Age* (Philadelphia: Westminster, 1975), 184.

29. Ibid., 187.

CHAPTER 7

1. Jacquelyn Grant, "The Sin of Servanthood," in Emilie Townes, ed., *A Troubling in My Soul: Womanist Perspectives on Evil and Suffering* (Maryknoll, N.Y.: Orbis, 1993), 200.

2. There are some creative poets and hymn-writers who are contributing to gender-inclusive language about God. I am thinking of Thomas Troeger, Ruth Duck, Brian Wren, and others. The most recent revisions of hymnals from the Presbyterian Church (USA), United Methodist Church, and United Church of Christ include these poets.

3. James Newton Poling, *Render Unto God: Economic Vulnerability, Family Violence, and Pastoral Theology* (St. Louis: Chalice, 2002), 246. The Lord's Prayer is printed by permission of the Wheadon United Methodist Church, Evanston, Ill., pastor Rev. Andres Ulman. This prayer has been developed over a period of years and used regularly in worship. It is an example of liturgical reform that comes from a practicing community rather than a scholar's mind.

4. Focus on the Family, Colorado Springs, Colo. 80995, http://www.focusonthefamily.com/, accessed March 3, 2011.

5. Bonnie Miller-McLemore, *Let the Children Come: Reimagining Childhood from a Christian Perspective* (San Francisco: Jossey-Bass, 2003); idem, *In the Midst of Chaos: Caring for Children as Spiritual Practice* (San Francisco: Jossey-Bass, 2006);

and Don S. Browning and Bonnie J. Miller-McLemore, eds., *Children and Child-hood in American Religions,* The Rutgers Series in Childhood Studies (New Brunswick, N.J.: Rutgers University Press, 2009).

6. Horace Bushnell, *Christian Nurture* (Grand Rapids: Baker, 1989 [1883]).

7. http://www.faithtrustinstitute.org, accessed March 3, 2011.

8. http://www.bmpcnc.org, accessed March 3, 2011.

9. Submitted by Linda Crockett, "Walking Together" program, Samaritan Counseling Center, Lancaster, Pennsylvania.

10. Robin J. Wilson, "Circles of Support and Accountability: A Canadian National Replication of Outcome Findings," *Sexual Abuse: A Journal of Research and Treatment* 21, no. 4 (2009): 412–30, http://nicic.gov/Library/021192, accessed March 3, 2011.

11. First Presbyterian Church, Evanston, Illinois, http://www.firstpresevanston.org/focusgroups/article193257.htm?img=1&imgsize=medium&imgalign=left &wraptext=1&body=1, accessed March 3, 2011.

12. Lutheran School of Theology in Chicago, Illinois, http://www.lstc.edu/greenzone/index.html, accessed March 3, 2011.

13. Trinity United Church of Christ, Chicago, Illinois, http://www.trinitychicago.org/index.php?option=com_frontpage&Itemid=1, accessed March 3, 2011.

CONCLUSION

1. Susan Marks, "The Need for Spirituality Rooted Compassion in My Life and in Sustainable Communities," *Creative Transformation* 18, no. 4 (Fall 2009): 19–20.

2. Carolina Bird Club, http://www.carolinabirdclub.org, accessed March 21, 2011.

3. Dean and Axel, eds., *The Size of God,* 46.

4. Harriett A. Jacobs, *Incidents in the Life of a Slave Girl,* ed. Jean Yellin Fagen (Cambridge: Harvard University Press, 1987). See my analysis in James Newton Poling, *Deliver Us From Evil: Resisting Racial and Gender Oppression* (Minneapolis: Fortress Press, 1996), 3–19.

5. Audre Lorde, "A Litany for Survival," in *The Black Unicorn: Poems* (New York: Norton, 1995), 31.

APPENDIX 1

1. James N. Poling, and Donald E. Miller, *Foundations for a Practical Theology of Ministry* (Nashville: Abingdon, 1985).

2. For example, the Roman Catholic Church, the Orthodox churches, and certain evangelical and Pentecostal groups do not ordain women to the most powerful offices such as pastor or priest.

3. For instance, 1 Corinthians 14:34-35: "Women should be silent in the churches. For they are not permitted to speak, but should be subordinate, as the law also says. If there is anything they desire to know, let them ask their husbands at home. For it is shameful for a woman to speak in church." This verse is important in some churches, but rejected by others as irrelevant for contemporary life.

See the resources by Christians for Biblical Equality, http://www.cbeinternational
.org/, accessed March 3, 2011.

4. "Practical Theology is critical, theological reflection on the practices of the
church as they interact with the practices of the world, with a view to ensuring
and enabling faithful participation in God's redemptive practices in, to, and for
the world." John Swinton and Harriett Mowat, *Practical Theology and Qualitative
Research Methods* (London: SCM, 2006), 5.

5. The Alban Institute, 2121 Cooperative Way, Suite 100, Herndon, VA
20171; (703) 964-2700; (800) 486-1318 (U.S. only), http://www.alban.org/,
accessed March 3, 2011.

APPENDIX 2

1. Edward Farley, *Theologia: The Fragmentation and Unity of Practical Theology*
(Philadelphia: Fortress Press, 1983).

2. Friedrich Schleiermacher, *Brief Outline of the Study of Theology* (Edinburgh:
T & T Clark, 1850 [1811]).

3. Edward Farley, "Interpreting Situations," in James N. Poling and Lewis
Mudge, eds., *Formation and Reflection: The Promise of Practical Theology* (Philadelphia: Fortress Press, 1987), 5.

4. In my own field of pastoral theology, the first articles appeared in the 1920s
and the first two books were published in 1936 by Anton Boisen and Russell Dicks.
Pastoral Psychology, founded in 1950, is our oldest continuous journal. Parallel
developments occurred in all of the discrete practical disciplines.

5. "The Association of Practical Theology (APT) archives contain a variety
of papers and minutes from the past six decades. Records from the Association of
Seminary Professors in the Practical Fields (ASPPF) constitute much of the material
available from years prior to 1984. APT records constitute much of the material
from 1984 forward. APT members have unlimited access to these records in the
form of downloadable and searchable PDFs. . . ." "[The] Fifth Biennial Meeting
of the Association of Seminary Professors in the Practical Fields, 1958" is the first
conference for which APT has records. See http://www.practicaltheology.org/index.
php?, accessed March 4, 2011.

6. International Academy of Practical Theology (http://www.ia-pt.org/); The
British and Irish Association for Practical Theology (http://www.biapt.org.uk/index.
shtml); United States Association of Practical Theology (http://www.practicaltheol-
ogy.org/); and *The International Journal of Practical Theology* (http://www.degruyter
.de/journals/ijpt/), all accessed March 4, 2011.

7. Twentieth-century founding texts include: James Poling and Lewis Mudge,
eds., *Formation and Reflection* (1987); James N. Poling and Donald E. Miller, *Foun-
dations for a Practical Theology of Ministry* (Nashville: Abingdon, 1985); Don S.
Browning, *Practical Theology: The Emerging Field in Theology, Church, and World*
(New York: Harper & Row, 1983); Edward Farley, *Theologia: The Fragmentation
and Unity of Practical Theology* (Philadelphia: Fortress Press, 1983); and Don S.
Browning, *A Fundamental Practical Theology: Descriptive and Strategic Approaches*
(Minneapolis: Fortress Press, 1995).

8. The Practical Theology Group of the American Academy of Religion describes its purpose as follows: "The Practical Theology Group engages practical theology and religious practice, reflects critically on religious traditions and practices, and explores issues in particular sub-disciplines of practical theology and ministry. The group engages this mission in five interrelated public spheres with the following goals: (1) For practical theology, to provide a national and international forum for discussion, communication, publication, and development of the field and its related sub-disciplines; (2) For theological and religious studies, to foster interdisciplinary critical discourse about religious practice, contextual research and teaching for ministry, and practical theological method and pedagogy; (3) For a variety of religious traditions, to enhance inquiry within a wide range of religions into religious practice and practical theology; (4) For academic pedagogy, to advance excellence in teaching and vocational development for faculty in divinity and seminary education generally and for graduate students preparing to teach in such settings; and (5) For the general public, to promote constructive reflection on social and cultural dynamics and implications of religious confession and practice." http://www.aarweb.org/Meetings/Annual_Meeting/Program_Units/PUinformation.asp?PUNum=AARPU151, accessed March 4, 2011.

9. Recent texts that summarize some of the issues of practical theology include: Elaine Graham, *Transforming Practice: Pastoral Theology in an Age of Uncertainty* (Eugene, Ore.: Wipf & Stock, 2002); and John Swinton and Harriet Mowat, *Practical Theology and Qualitative Research Methods* (London: SCM, 2006).

10. Poling and Miller, *Foundations*, 29–61.

11. This term is usually attributed to David Tracy, "The Task of Practical Theology," in Don S. Browning, ed., *Practical Theology: The Emerging Field in Theology, Church, and World* (New York: Harper & Row, 1983).

12. *Journal of Religion and Health*, http://www.springer.com/public+health/journal/10943, and the *Journal of Spirituality and Mental Health*, http://www.informaworld.com/smpp/title-content=t792306967-db=all, both accessed March 4, 2011.

13. Alvin Dueck and Kevin Reimer, *A Peaceable Psychology: Christian Therapy in a World of Many Cultures* (Grand Rapids: Brazos, 2009).

14. The understanding of nonpersons comes from Gustavo Gutiérrez; see James Poling and Elaine Graham, "Some Expressive Dimensions of a Liberation Practical Theology: Art Forms as Resistance to Evil," *International Journal of Practical Theology* 4, no. 2 (2000): 163–83.

15. See especially Graham, *Transforming Practices*; Rebecca Chopp, "Practical Theology and Liberation," in Poling and Mudge, eds., *Formation and Reflection*, 120–38; and Catherine Keller, Michael Nausner, and Mayra Rivera, eds., *Postcolonial Theologies: Divinity and Empire* (St. Louis: Chalice, 2004).

16. Itumelena J. Mosala, *Biblical Hermeneutics and Black Theology in South Africa* (Grand Rapids: Eerdmans, 1989).

17. Richard Osmer, *Practical Theology: An Introduction* (Grand Rapids: Eerdmans, 2008), 6.

18. This criticism of practical theology is developed in James Newton Poling, *The Abuse of Power: A Theological Problem* (Nashville: Abingdon, 1991), 186–91.

19. http://rescomp.stanford.edu/~cheshire/EinsteinQuotes.html, accessed on March 4, 2011.

20. I discuss this problem more in Poling, *The Abuse of Power*, chap. 9, 183–91.

21. See Poling and Miller, *Foundations for a Practical Theology of Ministry*, 62.

22. See James Newton Poling, *Render Unto God: Economic Vulnerability, Family Violence, and Pastoral Theology* (St. Louis: Chalice, 2002), 19.

23. See James Newton Poling, *Deliver Us from Evil: Resisting Racial and Gender Oppression* (Minneapolis: Fortress Press), xvi.

24. See Poling, *The Abuse of Power*, 187.

25. Poling and Miller, *Foundations for a Practical Theology of Ministry*, 62, 69.

26. The debate between Jürgen Habermas and Hans-Georg Gadamer has been prominent in practical theology because they explored the preunderstandings and socioeconomic structures affecting the identities of those who do research. See Browning, *A Fundamental Practical Theology*.

27. Don S. Browning, *Atonement and Psychotherapy* (Philadelphia: Westminster, 1966); idem, *Religious Thought and the Modern Psychologies* (Philadelphia: Fortress Press, 1987; 2d ed., 2000, with Terry D. Cooper); and idem, *Reviving Christian Humanism: The New Conversation on Spirituality, Theology and Psychology*, Theology and the Sciences (Minneapolis: Fortress Press, 2010).

28. Karl Barth, *The Humanity of God* (Louisville: Westminster John Knox, 1996 [1960]). See also William R. Garrett, "Troublesome Transcendence: The Supernatural in the Scientific Study of Religion," *Sociological Analysis* 35, no. 3 (Autumn 1974): 167–80.

29. David Tracy's term, "correlation of perspectives from culture and the Christian tradition," has been highly influential in practical theology. See Tracy, "Practical Theology in the Situation of Global Pluralism," in Poling and Mudge, eds., *Formation and Reflection*, 139–54. For more on the hermeneutical task, see Paul Ricoeur and John Thompson, *Hermeneutics and Human Sciences* (Cambridge: Cambridge University Press, 1981).

30. Theological ethics has an interesting relationship with practical theology. They are both responsible for making evaluative judgments about Christian life in the modern world and recommending patterns of action that are faithful to the gospel. However, the history of theological ethics has led it into a more philosophical direction that does not always attend to practice. Don S. Browning said that theological ethics should be the foundational basis for practical theology, but most practical theologians have not followed his lead. See Browning, *Foundations of Practical Theology*.

31. Rodney Hunter, "The Future of Pastoral Theology," *Pastoral Psychology* 29, no. 1 (Fall 1980): 58–69.

32. The following is adapted and revised from Poling, *The Abuse of Power*, 187–91.

33. "The elucidation of immediate experience is the sole justification for any thought; and the starting point for thought is the analytic observation of components of this experience. But we are not conscious of any clear-cut complete analysis of immediate experience, in terms of the various details which comprise its

definiteness. We habitually observe by the method of difference. Sometimes we see an elephant, and sometimes we do not. The result is that an elephant, when present, is noticed. Facility of observation depends on the fact that the object observed is important when present, and sometimes is absent." Alfred North Whitehead, *Process and Reality: An Essay in Cosmology* (New York: Free Press, 1978), 4. See also Ellen Wondra, "Theology in a Post-modern Key," *Plumbline* (December 1989): 4–16.

34. One critical theory that has most informed my work is psychoanalytic theory as reinterpreted by postmodern criticism, feminist theology, and black theology.

35. This section is heavily dependent on the constructive theology of Bernard Meland, *Essays in Constructive Theology: A Process Perspective* (Chicago: Exploration Press, 1988). "Within the Creative Passage there occurs the passage of history, not as a single stream, but as diverse cultural currents, each of which has its own dynamic structure, integrating through memory, precedent, custom and much more, the sequences of events and actualities that have constituted its living stream. The dynamic passage of events within each culture has given form to a *Structure of Experience* which can be said to be the enduring structural residue of the cultural history within its particular orbit of meaning, as seen from within the perspective of every present moment of that history. The Structure of Experience is thus the present immediacy within the total and inclusive Creative Passage. . . . Within each Structure of Experience there is to be found a persisting, elemental myth, giving shape to its cultural *mythos*, expressive of the hard-earned, endurable modes of response, subliminal for the most part, which have formed within that orbit of meaning" (5).

36. James Poling, "Empirical Theology," in *Dictionary of Pastoral Care and Counseling*, ed. Rodney Hunter (Nashville: Abingdon, 1990), 356–58.

37. Bernard Meland, *The Future of Empirical Theology* (Chicago: University of Chicago Press, 1969), 13, 297.

38. This insight comes from Marie Fortune, founder and director of Faith Trust Institute, Seattle, Washington.

Indexes
Scripture

Subjects and Authors